THE COMMERCIAL REAL ESTATE INVESTOR'S HANDBOOK:

A STEP-BY-STEP ROAD MAP TO FINANCIAL WEALTH

BY STEVEN FISHER

THE COMMERCIAL REAL ESTATE INVESTOR'S HANDBOOK: A STEP-BY-STEP ROAD MAP TO FINANCIAL WEALTH

Copyright © 2007 by Atlantic Publishing Group, Inc.
1405 SW 6th Ave. • Ocala, Florida 34471 • 800-814-1132 • 352-622-1875–Fax
Web site: www.atlantic-pub.com • E-mail: sales@atlantic-pub.com
SAN Number: 268-1250

ISBN-13: 978-1-60138-037-1   ISBN-10: 1-60138-037-2

Library of Congress Cataloging-in-Publication Data

Fisher, Steven D., 1944-
   The complete guide to commercial real estate investing : a step-by-step road map to financial wealth / by Steven Fisher.
      p. cm.
   ISBN-10: 1-60138-037-2 (alk. paper)
   ISBN-13: 978-1-60138-037-1
   1. Real estate investment. 2. Commercial real estate. I. Title.

   HD1382.5.F568 2007
   332.63'24--dc22
                    2007028213

EDITOR: Tracie Kendziora • tkendziora@atlantic-pub.com
INTERIOR LAYOUT DESIGN: Vickie Taylor • vtaylor@atlantic-pub.com
PROOFREADER: Angela Adams • aadams@atlantic-pub.com

Printed in the United States

Printed on Recycled Paper

CONTENTS

We recently lost our beloved pet "Bear," who was not only our best and dearest friend but also the "Vice President of Sunshine" here at Atlantic Publishing. He did not receive a salary but worked tirelessly 24 hours a day to please his parents. Bear was a rescue dog that turned around and showered myself, my wife Sherri, his grandparents Jean, Bob and Nancy and every person and animal he met (maybe not rabbits) with friendship and love. He made a lot of people smile every day.

We wanted you to know that a portion of the profits of this book will be donated to The Humane Society of the United States. *–Douglas & Sherri Brown*

The human-animal bond is as old as human history. We cherish our animal companions for their unconditional affection and acceptance. We feel a thrill when we glimpse wild creatures in their natural habitat or in our own backyard.

Unfortunately, the human-animal bond has at times been weakened. Humans have exploited some animal species to the point of extinction.

The Humane Society of the United States makes a difference in the lives of animals here at home and worldwide. The HSUS is dedicated to creating a world where our relationship with animals is guided by compassion. We seek a truly humane society in which animals are respected for their intrinsic value, and where the human-animal bond is strong.

Want to help animals? We have plenty of suggestions. Adopt a pet from a local shelter, join The Humane Society and be a part of our work to help companion animals and wildlife. You will be funding our educational, legislative, investigative and outreach projects in the U.S. and across the globe.

Or perhaps you'd like to make a memorial donation in honor of a pet, friend or relative? You can through our Kindred Spirits program. And if you'd like to contribute in a more structured way, our Planned Giving Office has suggestions about estate planning, annuities, and even gifts of stock that avoid capital gains taxes.

Maybe you have land that you would like to preserve as a lasting habitat for wildlife. Our Wildlife Land Trust can help you. Perhaps the land you want to share is a backyard—that's enough. Our Urban Wildlife Sanctuary Program will show you how to create a habitat for your wild neighbors.

So you see, it's easy to help animals. And The HSUS is here to help.

THE HUMANE SOCIETY OF THE UNITED STATES.

2100 L Street NW • Washington, DC 20037 • 202-452-1100

www.hsus.org

FOREWORD

By Jay Strike Carlin

Despite the challenges presented by commercial real estate investing, one can still profit handsomely when armed with the knowledge presented in this text. With this book in your library, you will be better equipped to deal with the nuances and challenges of commercial real estate investing. From smaller commercial structures to large office complexes and development projects, this text offers a glimpse into this exciting area and provides you with the knowledge necessary to succeed in commercial real estate investing.

Key components of the text guide you through getting started in commercial real estate investing, including tips on how to locate, fund, and develop these projects. Chapters on recognizing value in commercial real estate, which enlist various valuation approaches, including the cost approach, income approach, and market approach, will allow you to make proper and informed decisions on whether to invest or not. Other topics include the importance of identifying and securing proper funding for the purchase of commercial real estate. Pointers are provided to assist you in identifying suitable commercial real estate parcels and dealing with the various participants, including commercial real estate brokers, attorneys, funders, and others in the process.

Each aspect of commercial real estate investing is described and discussed in the text in easy to understand terms and is accompanied by examples. You do not have to be a commercial real estate professional to greatly benefit from the sage advice and clear examples used by the author.

Just like any other endeavor the rewards can be great if one studies lessons presented in the book and applies the knowledge contained within this well-written and complete text on the subject of commercial real estate. No commercial real estate investing professional should be without the knowledge gained in this book, which will help them become successful and grow their commercial projects from inception to completion.

Jay Strike Carlin, Esquire is a licensed attorney with an MBA, specializing in real estate acquisitions, development, and funding. He is the managing member of Strike, LLC, a real estate consulting firm focusing on commercial funding and development projects both domestic and international.

INTRODUCTION

Commercial real estate investing is investment in any property that produces income for you. Your investment can range in size from a duplex to large office buildings and industrial parks. Variety is one of the many advantages of investing in commercial real estate. Opportunities abound, such as fourplexes, strip malls, and multi-unit dwellings, so that once you decide to make a career in commercial real estate investing, you have choices among investment options. There are other advantages as well:

1) They offer ease of entry. Commercial real estate investing does not require a master's degree or a PhD. All it requires is a willingness to learn and a commitment to investment goals. In effect, you can create a prosperous future for yourself through hard work, dedication, and a willingness to learn all you can about the field of real estate.

2) They offer leverage, or the ability to use other people's money to finance your commercial real estate investments, meaning that you can use credit to finance a portion of the costs of purchasing or developing a real estate investment. Doing so allows you to get into the market by investing a minimum of your own capital. The key to leverage is to obtain funds at a lower cost than the return you get on your investments. Here is an example: Assume you invest $100,000 cash in a multi-unit dwelling. At the end of the first year, the cash flow from this investment is $15,000 after all operational expenses (tax, insurance, utilities, and so on) are accounted for. This means your return is 15 percent. A 15 percent return is not bad, but nothing compared to leverage. Here is how it works: Instead of investing $100,000, you invest only $20,000 in cash and borrow $80,000 from a lender. Graphically, the result looks like this:

Property's purchase price	$100,000
Lender's mortgage	- $80,000
Your cash investment	$20,000

Now, let us assume the annual cash flow from the property is $15,000, while the debt service (mortgage payment) is $7,000. Subtract $7,000 from $15,000, and you have $8,000 of money in your pocket as shown below:

Annual cash flow	$15,000
Mortgage payment	- $7,000
Money in your pocket	$8,000

This means the ROI (return on investment) on your $20,000 cash investment is 40 percent ($8,000 ÷ $20,000).

3) Commercial real estate investments offer good returns. On a historical basis, real estate has given investors in the United States an average annual return in the 8 to 10 percent range. This compares well with the average annual return of the stock market, especially when you consider that real estate does not have the volatility of the stock market. While commercial real estate is susceptible to economic cycles, it does not bounce up and down in value like stocks and bonds, and commercial real estate investments often generate greater returns than inflation, thus creating real wealth for you as an investor.

4) They provide long-term appreciation. A great strength of real estate investments is that they tend to increase in value over time, assuming they are well maintained, kept up to date, and managed effectively. On the whole real estate has consistently increased in value at a rate of about 6.1 percent on an annual basis. Appreciation has the wonderful effect of putting money in your pocket on a consistent long-term basis.

5) They produce income. In fact, compared to rental returns on single-family properties, they tend to produce a higher rental return. There is a good reason for this. For example, when you have a single-family property and it is vacant, it produces zero income until you find new occupants. However, when you own an apartment building with, say, 100 units, it is always producing income even when some vacancies occur. In addition, maintenance costs (on a per property basis) tend to be lower on commercial real estate properties than on single-family homes. Finally, appreciation on a commercial real estate investment, such as an apartment building, tends to be higher than on single-family homes because of sturdier construction and other factors.

6) They are a stable investment compared to the equities market. Unlike stocks and bonds, its value tends to be slow to rise and equally slow to fall. That means a commercial real estate investment is much more predictable than anything on Wall Street. Here is proof: Over the past three decades real estate values have gone up or down by about only 4 percent. During that same period of time, the stock market bounced up and down by nearly 17 percent in terms of daily risk. So, you can see that real estate can be a solid part of any investment portfolio.

7) They provide real tax benefits. The U.S. government gives you three tax advantages — deductibility, depreciation, and deferability. As an investor, you are allowed to *deduct* normal expenses, such as maintenance, improvement, property upkeep, and even mortgage interest, so that these deductions offset your investment income, reducing your tax bill. Federal tax laws also allow you to *depreciate* your investments, a mechanism to account for the normal "wear and tear" of a property, and they allow you to claim an annual decline in the value of a building. The net result is that you reduce your taxable income through depreciation at the same time the property is most likely appreciating in value. The third tax advantage is *deferability*. You can use the 1031 exchange mechanism to sell one property and buy another without incurring capital gains taxes. You simply have to re-invest all your profits into the next property (or properties) within a specific timeline. The use of the *Tax-Deferred 1031 Exchange* allows you to buy and sell investment real estate while deferring the taxes to a time when they will take a smaller bite out of your income. We will discuss this topic at more length later in the book.

8) Commercial real estate allows you to build wealth, one of the greatest advantages of the real estate field. As you gain properties, a synergistic effect occurs; that is, all the benefits mentioned above work together to create a whole greater than the sum of its parts. In basic terms, the longer you hold a property, the greater its equity grows while the mortgage payments decrease. In the meantime, you are receiving income and enjoying the benefits of depreciation, deductibility, and deferability. Investments do not get much better than this.

Of course, you need a hard-headed, common sense approach to commercial real estate investment, and that means recognizing its disadvantages as well. Every investment has its risks as well as its rewards, so it is wise to be aware of the risks so that you can manage them effectively.

The first risk of commercial real estate investment is *lack of knowledge.* This field is no place for amateurs. Lack of knowledge can cost you dearly in terms of poor investments. That is why it is often best to start small as you are learning and as your investments grow. You can gain knowledge in a variety of ways, such as "on-the-job" training, seminars, workshops, DVDs, or CDs, but one of the best ways is to find yourself a mentor who is willing to take the time to share knowledge from experience. You can do this by joining a firm specializing in such transactions, by having a real estate agent introduce you to other investors, or you can obtain a realtor's license of your own. A license provides you with credibility and proof that you have knowledge of the real estate market. At any rate, realize that learning is an ongoing requirement because markets, tax laws, and trends continually change. The investor who does not keep up with changes runs the risk of losing money or overlooking great investment opportunities. Make it your rule to continue learning.

The second potential disadvantage of commercial real estate investment is that *it requires capital.* Without capital, you will go nowhere despite what self-styled "gurus" tell you. "No money down" strategies simply do not work. You will be dealing with professionals, and they will want proof of capital. If you do not have it, they will show you the door. How do you acquire capital? There is no secret to it: Practice fiscal discipline.

Think of the long term and save every penny you have in your early investment years to build investment capital. Practicing fiscal discipline has another advantage: It teaches you to be just as hard-headed about money as the professionals you will be dealing with.

Experienced investors will respect you for your knowledge, and they will be willing to engage in deals that will be mutually beneficial. In basic terms, fiscal discipline means learning how to save, cut costs, and practice short-term sacrifice to gain long-term wealth and income.

A third potential disadvantage of commercial real estate is that *it ties up capital*. In other words, investment in property requires longer-term thinking than, say, the stock market. You cannot simply sell a property overnight as you can with shares in a publicly held corporation. That means you have to be able to carry the costs of a real estate investment over a longer period of time. Of course, with proper management of your capital, you can make sure you can meet these costs and wait to reap the rewards of your investment. It is all a matter of knowing the current market.

A fourth potential disadvantage of commercial real estate is *the effect of economic cycles*. A downturn in the economy can severely affect such investments as office buildings, commercial and industrial properties, and raw land. When such downturns occur, you can end up with investments that produce little or no income and which eat into your capital. Again, you can avoid this disadvantage by keeping up to date on current market conditions on local, regional, and national levels. Doing so will allow you to invest judiciously and save your capital for a time when an upturn in the economy signals that new opportunities are available.

A fifth potential disadvantage of commercial real estate is *higher risk*. The larger the real estate investment, the larger the risk. Professional investors never lose their cool and fall in love with a property. Instead, they objectively analyze every deal in terms of market conditions, potential income, building condition, and the intrinsic value of property. If the numbers do not add up, they gracefully exit and look for other deals.

In the next chapter, we will look at all the types of commercial properties and their advantages and disadvantages so that you can set goals for your financial future.

CHAPTER 1

TYPES OF COMMERCIAL REAL ESTATE INVESTMENTS

Commercial real estate properties can range from small to immense. Each type has advantages and disadvantages. Our advice is to study each type in this chapter closely so you can make an informed decision as to your investment goals. But first, let us examine an investment opportunity to help you build toward a career in commercial real estate.

APARTMENT BUILDINGS

Apartment buildings are not considered commercial properties; however, we include them in this chapter because they are a logical first step on the path to ownership of many single-family homes and investment in commercial properties. Apartment buildings are a logical choice for several reasons.

One, they generate cash flow for you from the start. That cash flow may be small in the beginning; however, as time passes, it will increase to build your investment capital because the mortgage expense stays fixed while your rents rise faster than expenses.

Two, one apartment building is much easier to manage and maintain than several single-family homes; after all, you concentrate on a single property rather than running back and forth to several.

Three, an apartment building appreciates faster than single-family homes because it costs more in the first place. A single-family home worth $300,000 appreciating at 10 percent generates $30,000 worth of appreciation. An apartment building worth $1,000,000 will generate $100,000 worth of appreciation at 10 percent, meaning more cash in your pocket.

Four, an apartment building allows you to charge for amenities and services, such as coin-operated laundries, lawn care, parking, pet fees, and storage. These amenities and services generate extra revenue that you can invest in larger commercial properties.

As with any investment, there are potential negatives. With an apartment building, many of the headaches lie in management and upkeep. If you manage the property yourself, you will have to deal with the needs of tenants — garbage disposal breakdowns and complaints about lack of parking. You will have to do paperwork, fill vacancies, and keep the grounds neat and clean.

However, if you plan on being a serious investor in commercial real estate, you should not be taking on these tasks. Your jobs are to seek out new, profitable investments and to think big. Remember, daily management and maintenance are important, but they are not going to make money. That is why you should hire a property manager as soon as it is practical so that you can concentrate on acquiring properties that will build wealth and a secure future.

COMMERCIAL PROPERTIES

In our definition, commercial real estate includes a variety of industrial, office, and retail properties, such as grocery stores, office buildings, raw land, self-storage, retail space, and strip malls. The variety is a great asset to potential investors; it means they have a wide variety of opportunities. Learn as much as you can about each type and specialize in the one that fits your personality and financial resources. For example, if you are a "nuts and bolts" person, you might enjoy working with customers in the industrial market. On the other hand, if you are an urban individual who wears a suit and tie every day, you may prefer the office building market. The descriptions below will give you a start in analyzing your fit with specific commercial real estate properties. However, before we do that, here is a brief overview of key concepts we will be exploring at more length later in the book:

- **Key Concept 1:** Know everything about the investment area. Be sure to check out supply and demand (see Key Concepts 2 and 3 below). Ask yourself questions like, "How much total space is available for rent?" "What is the price per square foot?" "What are the vacancy rates and the rate of change in those rates over time?" "What are the traffic patterns?"

- **Key Concept 2:** Seek positive absorption, which is a situation where the demand for space is greater than the supply, driving property and rental rates up. If you are in early, you profit.

- **Key Concept 3:** Avoid *negative* absorption, where the supply of space is too great. As a result, vacancies increase, rents fall, and you end up with the short end of the investment stick.

Now that you know the key concepts, let us study specific markets.

Office Buildings

An office building's size depends on the local population. Large, new office buildings are often referred to as "Class A" buildings in real estate because they are located on expensive land in urban areas. For your reference, all classifications are listed below as shown in our companion book *The Complete Guide to Real Estate Options*.

OFFICE BUILDING CLASSIFICATIONS

- **Class A Building** — The highest quality, newer, large buildings that have up-to-date amenities, such as telecommunication/Internet capabilities, and are located in desirable areas.
- **Class B Building** — This classification describes an average building, one that may be more than ten years old, with many amenities and located in a desirable area.
- **Class C Building** — A term commonly used to describe a below average building. It may be an older, well-maintained building but have smaller units. Class C buildings are typically located in stable areas.
- **Class D Building** — These are older buildings that have high vacancy rates, lack of maintenance, few amenities, and are often located in or near marginal areas.

Office buildings attract clients based on their design and available space. They can be profitable, but their large size means you need large amounts of capital to buy and maintain them, so you may need to combine resources with other investors. The cost may limit opportunities to institutional investors or Real Estate Investment Trusts (REITs).

Retail

This category can include everything from "mom and pop" stores to national chains. Here is an overview of the most common types, listed in alphabetical order:

"Big Box" Stores

The term "big box" refers to the powerful, international discount chains, such as Wal-Mart and Target. Their nickname comes from their large size, anywhere from 200,000 square feet to 1,000,0000-plus square feet. If you are a beginner in commercial real estate investment, big box stores are not for you. They can be profitable, but they are most often handled by experienced and sophisticated investors who have the means to put together million-dollar deals.

Large Shopping Centers

Such centers most often have national chains as tenants and one or more anchors that draw large numbers of customers. The "mega mall" in the Minneapolis-St. Paul area with 4.2 million square feet is the largest shopping center in the United States. Often, large shopping centers have "anchors" that draw customer traffic. Anchors are national chain stores or tenants like Sears or JC Penney. Large shopping centers are not open to the general pool of real estate investors.

Strip Malls

Like the big box stores, these plazas are everywhere. They are smaller and often occupy highly visible corner locations with high drive-by traffic. Unlike large shopping malls, they do not have anchors to draw a lot of customers. Instead, strip malls tend to attract small businesses such as restaurants, dance studios, and convenience stores without the financial muscle of national chains. The upside of investment in strip malls is that they can be profitable when properly managed. The downside is that such investment carries more risk because small tenant operations are dependent on the business acumen of the individual owners. If the tenants are not financially astute and good managers, they can go out of business quickly, leaving you with an empty space that needs to be filled. Also, if traffic patterns change in a drastic manner (road construction, re-routing), customers can vanish. This type of investment requires careful analysis of the neighborhood to determine its advantages and disadvantages.

Keep in mind that there are many different types of retail properties available that are not covered in this section. You will have to study your market carefully to discover what specific opportunities are available.

RAW LAND

Undeveloped land can be a good investment if you buy it in the *path of progress*. The term "path of progress" refers to an area that is going to expand with new businesses and residential homes. If you get in early, you are assured of good returns on your investment, especially if a major company (distribution center, IT center) decides to build on property you own. On the other hand, if you guess wrong, you have got money tied up in land doing nothing for you, possibly for a long time. In the meantime, you must pay property taxes and liability insurance, while keeping the land maintained in an attractive manner for potential investors.

There is another disadvantage: Lenders tend to see raw land as a speculative investment. As a result, they demand higher down payments (generally in the 30 to 40 percent range) and charge higher fees and interest rates. Finally, undeveloped land has no tax depreciation write-offs.

INDUSTRIAL

Industrial investments can range from the traditional "dirty" businesses (chemicals, petroleum, and steel) to the modern "clean" industries (computers and electronics). Often, such properties are concentrated in business and industrial "parks." Business parks hold the clean industries (distribution centers, medical manufacturing, electronic manufacturing) while industrial parks hold the dirty industries (traditional manufacturers and distribution centers). Of the two, the business parks tends to have higher values since they attract service businesses (banks, restaurants) to serve the greater population of office workers. Often, the best investments in business or industrial parks tend to be "multi-use" buildings that will hold several different tenants as opposed to "special purpose" buildings. The reason is that special purpose buildings are designed to meet the particular needs of the tenant (a bank, a restaurant). Therefore, if a tenant decides to leave, you are faced with finding the same kind of lessee or paying the cost of converting the building to a different use. With a multi-purpose building, you do not face this possibility. It means you incur a lower risk of vacancy and greater assurance that your revenue stream will continue to flow.

Large commercial real estate projects include master-planned communities and urban renewal projects that are not open to the average investor. They require massive amounts of capital and the ability to work smoothly with several different interested parties — investors, city governments, communities, and politicians, so you need to be an experienced and sophisticated investor. If you are a beginner in the commercial real estate market, you may want to consider large projects as a long-range goal, or if you have the funds available, you can always join other investors to form a pool of capital, allowing you to gain entry and spread the risk.

CHAPTER 2

THE BASICS OF GETTING STARTED

In the last chapter, we defined the types of commercial real estate investments available. Now it is time to take the first and most important part of becoming an investor: setting goals. Goal-setting is a trait of all successful people. Entrepreneurs, investors, scientists, athletes, statesmen — you name a successful person, and he or she has set goals to make major achievements in their lives. They set a clear course that allows them to stay on the path to success because they establish a tangible vision in their minds.

Goals have other benefits. They allow you to measure your progress against specific objectives so you know what progress you have made. Therefore, you can enjoy successes as they occur and derive the motivation to "keep on keeping on." There are many methods of setting goals. In this chapter, we will provide you with one of the best — the SMART system.

Before you set goals, however, you will have to answer some important questions to be able to choose your investment path. The answers will set a general course for the future.

- Do I want to make commercial real estate investment a full-time career?

- Do I want to make commercial real estate investment a part-time career as part of a long-range investment strategy?

- Do I want to become a commercial real estate speculator?

The answers to these questions will drive your goals. Of course, you can start your career as a part-time investor and move to full-time status or become a speculator. There are no hard and fast rules to becoming an investor. (See the next chapter, Career Options, for strategies to pursue.) However, you do need to start somewhere and set goals from the beginning. Let us assume you want to be a full-time investor and are new to the field.

THE SMART METHOD OF SETTING GOALS

The SMART name is an acronym for specific characteristics of setting effective goals:

S = Specific

M = Measurable

A = Action-oriented

R = Realistic

T = Timely

Let us look at each of these characteristics in depth.

S = Specific

Any goal you set should always be specific, not general. General goals tend not to get accomplished since they are vague. "I plan to become a commercial real estate investor" is an example of a vague goal. It does not state what type of investor you want to be or what types of investments you want to specialize in. A more specific goal would be, "I plan to become a full-time commercial real estate investor specializing in retail properties." This goal gives you focus and direction.

M = Measurable

Any goal you set should be measurable. You should be able to answer questions like, "How much? How many? How will I know I have accomplished the goal?" For example, the goal, "I want to learn all I can about commercial real estate investment" is not a measurable goal. It does not state any specifics about how you will obtain that knowledge. A measurable goal would look like this: "I will begin my education in commercial real estate investment by taking courses in real estate at XYZ College" or "I will begin my education in commercial real estate investment by taking a job as a leasing agent with Bob Smith at Smith Realty."

A = Action-Oriented

This refers to the steps you take to achieve a goal. By action-oriented, we mean that each step should be an actual, physical action. For example, we mentioned the goal of studying real estate at XYZ College. The first, action-oriented step would be to contact the XYZ admissions office to discuss enrollment options and dates. Therefore, you could write the step as, "Call or e-mail XYZ admissions office to discuss curriculum by April 1." This is a simple step that gets you into action.

R = Realistic

You should set goals that are high, but realistic. For example, the goal, "I want to earn $500,000 in my first year as a real estate leasing agent" is most likely not realistic if you are new to the field. A more realistic goal would be, "In my first year as a leasing agent, I will acquire the skills and knowledge necessary to earn X number of dollars and establish a basis for increasing my income by X percent in following years." This kind of goal demonstrates realistic thinking and long-range planning.

T = Timely

Every goal needs a completion date. A specific date keeps you from procrastinating or getting off track. Examples of timely goals include: "I will complete my curriculum by May." "I will complete due diligence on the strip mall property by January 10." "I will have financing in place by September."

The SMART method of goals is one you can use throughout your career to stay on track, and we highly recommend you use it or one similar to it. You will find its rewards are vast.

Let us assume you have established the goal of becoming a full-time commercial real estate investor and used the SMART method to determine specific steps to achieve that goal. Now it is time to take a look at the resources available for your plan. This calls for some hard-headed analysis of your financial resources and your level of real estate knowledge.

ANALYSIS OF YOUR CURRENT FINANCIAL POSITION

Whether it is to pay for a degree in business or to invest money in a particular property, you need to know what your finances are. Simply put, do you have the cash reserves to become a full-time real estate investor? Remember, investment calls for money on hand to handle delays or setbacks.

So-called "gurus" will tell that there is an easy way to wealth. This is nonsense. The path calls for hard work, common sense, and an unswerving dedication to the craft of investment. Therefore, unless you are blessed with a high income or receive a windfall from a relative, you will need to scrimp and save to accumulate the capital to achieve your dream. Below are the steps to take to accumulate that capital.

Budgeting

If you do not know what your current income and expenses are, how can you expect to handle the more complex financial analysis required for real estate investment? Therefore, the first step to take is to create a budget analysis. If you find that you are spending too much and not saving enough, it is time to cut back on discretionary spending. Stop eating out so much. Rent videos instead of going to movies. Avoid designer clothing. Brew your own coffee instead of popping out for that expensive latte. There are many ways to cut costs and save money. Preparing a monthly budget and adhering to it will set you on the path of substantial accumulation of capital.

Credit Card Debt

Use of credit cards is the downfall of many American families. They are so easy to use and convenient, but the interest and fees for late payments take money out of your pocket. Therefore, if you have credit card debt, your immediate task is to eliminate that debt. Pay off the highest-interest cards first, of course.

If you have several credit cards in your wallet or purse, get rid of as many as possible and stick with one or two with the lowest interest rates. Of course, do not forget to reduce or eliminate other debts as well, such as furniture loans and car loans. Remember the golden rule of financial security: **Pay yourself first**. If paying off debt is difficult for you, make it easier by keeping your eyes on the prize — a great and profitable future in commercial real estate investment. The ability to think long range and maintain financial discipline is a prime characteristic of successful investors in the real estate market.

Financial Knowledge

A third step to take is to get a financial education, particularly if you are planning on being a full-time investor. A fundamental knowledge of financial documents, such as profit and loss statements, balance sheets, and operating statements, is necessary. These will not be needed at the basic level of lease options, but they will be valuable when moving into more complex areas of real estate. Financial knowledge will enable you to leverage the initial lease option transactions into greater profitability and a secure future.

ANALYSIS OF YOUR KNOWLEDGE

Knowledge is power in the real estate market. Ignorance can stop your career quickly. Therefore, your first priority should be to learn all aspects of real estate and make learning an ongoing process. It can be a "learn on the job" education or a college education. The method of learning does not matter as long as you learn. Our advice is to analyze your current knowledge in an objective manner. Identify strengths you can build on and weaknesses you need to eliminate or improve. This can be done through a personal SWOT analysis. Originally designed for the audit of organizations, it can be applied to individuals as well. The term "SWOT" is an acronym for "Strengths, Weaknesses, Opportunities, and Threats."

Strengths	Weaknesses
Opportunities	Threats

In the grid, you list items under each heading. For example, in the "Strengths" grid, you might list "financial, sales, and local market knowledge." In the "Weaknesses" grid, you might list "lack of experience, capital, and a mentor." These two grids allow you to list personal factors you need to consider. The other two grids permit you to list *external* factors. For example, under the "Opportunities" heading, you might list "expanding retail market, path of progress in Apple Valley neighborhood, indications big box stores are interested in our town." Under the "Threats" heading, you might list "fierce competition with fatter wallets than I have, national economy is uncertain and could affect local market." 29

Therefore, a partially completed example would look like the grid below:

Strengths		Weaknesses	
1.	Financial knowledge	1.	Lack of experience in real estate field
2.	Sales experience	2.	Lack of capital
3.	Knowledge of local market	3.	Lack of mentor
4.	_____	4.	_____
5.	_____	5.	_____
6.	_____	6.	_____
7.	_____	7.	_____
8.	_____	8.	_____
9.	_____	9.	_____
10.	_____	10.	_____
Opportunities		**Threats**	
1.	Expanding retail market, path of progress in Apple Valley neighborhood	1.	Fierce competition with fatter wallets than I have
2.	Indications big box stores are interested in our town	2.	National economy is uncertain and could affect local market
3.	_____	3.	_____
4.	_____	4.	_____
5.	_____	5.	_____
6.	_____	6.	_____
7.	_____	7.	_____
8.	_____	8.	_____
9.	_____	9.	_____
10.	_____	10.	_____

ANALYSIS OF YOUR MINDSET

Investment in commercial real estate is essentially an entrepreneurial venture. As such, it requires the entrepreneurial spirit to be successful in the field. Some believe entrepreneurs are made, not born. They are utterly mistaken. While it is true that a few individuals seem blessed with an extraordinary amount of entrepreneurial talent, 99 percent of entrepreneurs achieved their success through hard work, dedication, and discipline. In other words, they were not born entrepreneurs; they made themselves into entrepreneurs. Deliberately or instinctively, some do a SWOT analysis on themselves as entrepreneurs and build on their strengths and work to improve their weaknesses. Others look to role models in different fields to see what the common characteristics of successful people are and then develop those characteristics in themselves. This latter strategy saves time and a lot of trial and error. Below is a list of the common characteristics of successful entrepreneurs in any field. Review it to see where your strengths lie and to pinpoint areas that need to be improved. As you review, remember that all these characteristics can be learned.

Clear-Cut Goals

We discussed goals earlier in the chapter, but it bears repeating here that there is one universal characteristic of entrepreneurs: the ability to formulate clear goals and then commit to achieving them. They realize that goals give them clarity and keep them on the road to success. Entrepreneurs use long- and short-range goals to stay on task. They also do not think of their goals as something abstract to consult every now and then; instead, they think of their goals as concrete and real and refer to them every day.

A Positive Mental Attitude

Some people are natural optimists; others are not. The mistake made by many less optimistic individuals is to believe that they cannot develop a positive mental attitude — an absolute requirement for entrepreneurship. Nothing is further from the truth. You can develop a positive outlook on life. You can do this in several ways. First, set goals as described earlier in the chapter. Goals give you definite, positive targets to aim for and push negatives out of your mind.

Another method that can be used to gain and maintain optimism is the use of "affirmations" or "positive assertions." As explained in a companion book, *The Complete Guide to Real Estate Options, What Smart Investors Need to Know — Explained Simply*, affirmations are simple statements that can be written down on Post-It® Notes and then pasted in strategic places. In effect, the brain can be reprogrammed into positive channels with statements like:

- "Today, I'm one step closer to obtaining financing for the mall property."

- "Failures never stop me; they only motivate me."

- "I will achieve financial security for me and my family."

- "I did a great job on that office building deal."

Notice that the affirmations above are both general and specific (in relation to real estate). The most powerful motivations are the ones that are specific to your own life. We recommend choosing this course. If you have trouble coming up with them at first, go on the Internet and type "affirmations examples" into the search window. This action will provide many examples to serve as a basis for other statements. There are many spots to place these reminders. Examples are:

- Bathroom mirror
- Car dashboard

- Dresser mirror
- Home/office desk
- Closet door
- Refrigerator door
- Computer monitor
- Wallet
- Front door
- Briefcase
- Telephone
- Books

Use your imagination and find different places to put the affirmations.

Another method of achieving optimism is a simple one — stay away from people with bad attitudes. Avoid whiners and nay-sayers. Such people only live in the past and will slow you down or divert you from your course completely. Consciously or unconsciously, their aim in life is to bring others down to their level, stuck in an endless cycle of self-recrimination and blame. It is a waste of your valuable time.

Personal Strengths

The ability to focus on personal strengths goes hand-in-hand with a positive mental attitude. That is why, earlier in the chapter, we recommended the use of the SWOT analysis. This technique is useful because many of us are trained by our culture to focus on our weaknesses. Avoid this mindset — it is a dismal swamp of negativity. Instead, focus on your strengths and use them as your "success leverage." This does not mean that you have to be a "Pollyanna" and see everything through rose-colored glasses. Instead, it pays to be as objective as possible about your strengths and weaknesses. If you have a weakness, do not dwell on it — do something to improve or eliminate it. For example, if your presentation skills are not strong, take a class in making business presentations. If you are not a polished speaker, join Toastmasters to tap into a supportive organization. If you feel you are not as smart as the next person, remember you do not need to be a genius to succeed in the commercial real estate market; you only need to be disciplined and dedicated. Good, old-fashioned sweat accomplishes more in the real estate world than genius.

Lastly, be aware that you may have strengths or weaknesses you are not aware of. How do you discover what they are? Simple — ask others. Ask friends, family, and business colleagues to tell you what they feel are your strengths and your areas for improvement. Write down the results and then use the list to figure out how to build on personal strengths and reduce or eliminate weaknesses.

Self-Motivation

Another common characteristic of entrepreneurs is their ability to motivate themselves. They are self-starters in every sense of the word and realize that action is the key to success. Procrastination is a word that is not even in their vocabulary. They do not waste time on tasks that are not directly related to their goals. They think long-range and are willing to sacrifice in the short-term to achieve success.

Perseverance

Sheer doggedness is another valuable entrepreneurial characteristic to develop. In essence, successful entrepreneurs never, ever give up. They do not care how many obstacles they run into or how much negativity they face; they simply plow ahead. This is an extremely valuable trait to develop in the world of commercial real estate investment because you are going to face skepticism from lenders, investors, and others who do not share your vision. By combining persistence with sound business planning, you can overcome this skepticism and make your vision come true.

Be aware that skepticism may come from an unexpected source — your family or friends. In the case of family, doubt may arise from fear; your spouse may simply be scared of the new direction you are taking and feel his or her security is threatened. The best way to handle this is to keep him or her informed right from the start of your plans. Do not simply come home one day and announce, "I'm going to become a commercial real estate investor." That kind of action is not fair to your family and will create a climate of insecurity. Instead, work with your family and let them know that they are an integral part of any future plans. Once they know you value and trust their input, they will be on board and provide valuable support. In the case of friends, jealousy can occur. They may resent your independent spirit and, consciously or unconsciously, try to undermine your efforts with statements like, "That's pretty risky, isn't it?" or "I heard about a case where so-and-so lost his shirt in real estate." In other words, they are inviting you to give up so they can feel better about themselves. Do not accept the invitation. Simply say, "That's interesting," and stick to your goals. Remember, little people do not accomplish great things.

A Deep Commitment to Learning

We mentioned learning earlier in relation to the SWOT analysis, but we want to re-emphasize its importance here. Commercial real estate is an ever-evolving field with changes in laws, local, and national market conditions, and ignorance of these changes can cost you money. So, it makes sense to commit to learning on a continual basis. There is also the flip side — knowledge can make you much more money. The more expertise you gain, the more income you can earn. In addition, expertise gains you respect, and respect brings in more clients and deals. Simply put, learning is an investment in a secure and enjoyable financial future.

Commitment to Success in All Aspects of Life

Entrepreneurs are "pragmatic altruists." That is, they want success for everybody in their lives — family, business associates, the community, and so on. Their reasons are both selfless and practical. First, wishing for success for everyone in your life is the right thing to do. Second, they know that by spreading and sharing success they stand to gain practical rewards for their efforts; the more success they spread, the greater their standing in the community and the more people want to deal with them. The result — increased business and reputation.

Ethical Behavior

You may believe that, as a commercial real estate investor, your greatest asset might be your ability to put deals together or to organize a project. While those abilities are important, they are still not the most important for a long-term career in real estate. The most important is your reputation. Many commercial deals involve a lot of money, and investors and others want to deal with honest people. Sure, you hear stories about greedy or unethical characters in the news, but the reason you hear about them is that their stupidity leads them to jail or fines or both. They have very short careers. So, it is not only morally right to build and maintain a reputation for ethical behavior, but it also makes good business sense. It is an investment in your financial future, plus you will have the satisfaction of gaining respect from everyone in your life.

Happiness

This entrepreneurial characteristic may surprise you. Most people have an image of entrepreneurs as driven, mono-maniacs who are often so obsessive that they fail to enjoy life. The opposite is true in most cases. True entrepreneurs love what they do. They do not even consider their "jobs" as jobs. They pursue projects for fun as well as profit. They seek happiness in every aspect of their lives. This does not mean entrepreneurs engage in rosy-colored thinking. Often, they are hard-headed realists and know challenges will arrive. The difference between them and the average person is that they love facing those challenges and overcoming them. It is a test of their determination and skill. In short, it is fun for them. So, we recommend that you seek this type of entrepreneurial happiness in commercial real estate investment as well.

A PROJECT MANAGER MENTALITY

One of the paradoxes of being an entrepreneur within the commercial real estate investment field is that you not only have to have a leadership mentality, but you also have to have a project manager mentality as well. That is, you have to have a clear, strategic vision and be "tactical" or detail-oriented at the same time so as to achieve that vision. Without attention to detail, your vision of a project is not accomplished on time and within budget or, in extreme cases, is not accomplished at all.

In the classic corporate sense, the definition of a project manager is that he or she coordinates all aspects of a project and is responsible for finding the people and resources to bring it to a successful completion. In the entrepreneurial sense, it means you assume responsibility for getting things done no matter what obstacles are placed in your path. Essentially, you are a problem-solver and a solution-seeker.

You may already have a project-management mindset, but, if you do not, do not worry — the skills are easy to learn. Even better, you can apply these skills to every aspect of your life, not just commercial real estate. They teach you to set priorities and balance your life so you end up accomplishing more in less time. That, in turn, reduces stress and creates more enjoyment of work, family, and life.

We mentioned the "corporate" definition of a project manager above; that is, a person who manages projects within a corporation. As an investor and entrepreneur, you will share many of those characteristics, but your role will have a different flavor to it. Below, we have provided an overview of the essential traits you need to develop in order to carry out successful investment projects.

The first trait is *knowledge of the project*. This may sound obvious, but you need to have mastery of a particular investment in order to be credible with everyone involved — partners, lenders, construction firms, and so on. If you are not credible, you will not have respect. Others will lack trust in you and be reluctant to put their money on the line. This does not mean you have to be an expert in every aspect of a development project (although it helps), but you do have to know enough to set assignments and point team members in the right direction. Without clear direction from you, those team members may struggle due to lack of direction. The result may be cost overruns and potential failure. In a nutshell, you need to be the "go-to" person — the one who solves problems and keeps the project "train" on the tracks.

The second trait is *the ability to anticipate change and manage it*. It is no secret that change is a constant in life and in business projects — change in zoning laws, project specifications, personnel, money, and so on. As mentioned previously, entrepreneurs love the challenge of meeting change. So, we recommend that you adopt the same attitude. Think of it as an opportunity to exercise your creativity and learn lessons you can apply in the future.

The third trait to cultivate is to *be a relationship builder*. Any successful investment is the result of creating smooth relationships with all the parties involved. And smooth relationships are built by letting team members know that you value their opinions, their expertise, and their skills. The old saying, "You catch more flies with honey than with vinegar" applies here. So, always seek to build positive relationships with everyone involved in your investment projects. It will not always be easy at times, but, in the long run, things will run more smoothly and profits will result. Excellent relationships also result in people wanting to do more projects with you, so they are well worth building to increase future success.

The fourth trait is more of a warning than a characteristic — *do not get lost in technical details at the cost of the desired end result*. This may sound contradictory, but if you are a very technically-oriented person, you may tend to lose sight of your ultimate goal — a profitable project. So, do not forget to pay attention to such important items as partner/investor relationships, the productivity of contractors, the market, and so on. In essence, you have to keep one idea on your overall vision while keeping a sharp focus on the steps necessary to carry out a successful project.

CHAPTER 3

CAREER OPTIONS

In the previous chapter, you were asked to complete a SMART action plan to determine your goals and objectives for commercial real estate investment. This chapter will provide you with an overview of the paths you can take so you can more clearly articulate those goals and objectives. One of the wonderful things about real estate is that there is a wide range of properties and options from which to choose. In other words, you can find an investment strategy to fit your individual needs. You may want to make commercial real estate investment a full-time career. You may want to keep your job and adopt a long-term investment strategy. Or you may want to speculate. Let us look at each of these options in turn.

A FULL-TIME CAREER

Most individuals do not start investment in commercial real estate in their first year of business. They simply do not have the money to be a player in the game and do not understand the subtle rules of the trade. One option is to hire an experienced leasing agent in a local commercial firm as an assistant. Because they are on the inside, assistants learn the basic and subtle details of investment in the commercial market. More important, they tap into a network of investors and start the process of building their own network. By working hard and diligently, they start with small investments and work their way up into large and more profitable ones. Another option is to begin in the residential market and buy single-family homes. With astute management, an investor can earn a good cash-flow, make a good profit, and move up to the next level — multi-unit dwellings (fourplexes, apartments). He or she can then use the cash flow or sale of these properties to gain entry into the commercial market. This is a great way to learn real estate investment as you go. The risks are lower in the residential and multi-unit markets, and you can gain experience that will be invaluable once you enter the area of commercial investment.

A PART-TIME INVESTMENT CAREER

Many people keep their jobs and invest in real estate as part of a long-term investment strategy. They use the residential-investment strategy described above. Building upon equity in their own home(s), they buy rental properties and become landlords. If they invest astutely and grow their portfolio, eventually they may have to make a decision — stick with the current job or become full-time investors.

A SPECULATION CAREER

Speculation in commercial real estate has the advantage of allowing you to invest little money in order to obtain good, or even huge, gains. One way to speculate is with options to purchase. This is a long-term strategy. Here is an example: Assume you have studied your local community and identified the "path of progress" (an area showing future growth). You know there is a lot of potential, so you offer to buy an option on a parcel of land, betting that the value will increase dramatically over a period of time, say, five to ten years. So, you offer $7,500 (or the appropriate amount) for a five-year option to buy the property at the current value with annual option extension payments. Essentially, you have locked in a current price, and then, when the parcel appreciates in value, you can buy it and either resell it at a higher price or keep it yourself for development. In other words, for a minimum investment you have gained a great profit. The downside of options is that your capital is not protected. There is always the possibility that you might not be able to resell the property, and it ends up as an albatross around your neck. However, if you do your homework carefully, this scenario can be avoided, and a good profit can be made.

Another speculative strategy is called "flipping." Flipping is a quick turnover method. It involves buying an option on a piece of property and then turning around and selling that option to another buyer for a profit. Let us return to the "path of progress" for an example to illustrate how flipping works. Through due diligence, you have found a residential area that is slowly turning commercial. So, you identify a residential lot that has the potential for re-zoning for commercial use and buy a one-year option to buy that lot. Then, you seek out buyers (or they seek you out) who see the potential for re-zoning and sell the option to them. Without ever having taken property of the title, you have resold the option and turned a nice profit. Often, the "simultaneous closing" technique is used in flipping. That is, you buy and resell the property in escrow at virtually the same time on the day of closing.

A "rollover" strategy is similar to flipping. The difference is that the transaction is part of a development deal right from the start. There is a one to two year escrow period at the start of such deals. Within this time frame, you want the best possible price for your land, as the seller. The buyer needs the time to gather all the project elements together and get rezoning accomplished. As the seller, you also need to get all approvals and lease the project (to break-even occupancy) while simultaneously offering the project for sale. This strategy provides the buyer the option of building the project as planned or rolling the money over without risk. For you, as the seller, you can make a handsome profit without ever having taken title of the property.

From this chapter, you can see that you have a number of options to pursue. Which option you choose depends upon your individual needs, temperament, and financial situation.

CHAPTER 4

FUNDAMENTAL FACTORS AFFECTING COMMERCIAL REAL ESTATE VALUES

No doubt you have heard the common saying that there are three important factors to consider when buying real estate — location, location, location. Well, location is an important factor, but there are other, equally important ones to consider, particularly in the area of commercial real estate. This chapter will acquaint you with all the factors you need to take into account when considering the purchase of property.

LOCATION

If you are a beginning investor, our advice is to start locally because it is likely that you already know something about the area. This knowledge gives you a jump start and makes it much easier for you to search for properties and visit them because they are within easy driving distance. An added benefit is that starting locally keeps your costs down; you do not have to travel long distances or pay for gas, food, and lodging. Therefore, start with your base knowledge of the local area and then add to that base by learning everything you can about it; for example, types of industries and property values. It is a simple equation; the more educated you become about the market, the better you will be at spotting opportunities, evaluating them, and making sound deals.

A fundamental part of locating good commercial properties is to identify growing areas. They are an indication of a healthy, expanding economy. In real estate terms, this is called "the path of progress," and you definitely want to identify that path because there are several, important benefits. First, property values trend upward in these areas. Second, it is easier to find and keep good tenants for retail and office businesses in particular, and that, in turn, means occupancy is higher and turnover is lower. For you, it can all add up to a higher revenue stream. From our companion book, *The Real Estate Investor's Handbook: The Complete Guide for the Individual Investor* (Atlantic Publishing Company, **www.atlantic-pub.com**), here are the guidelines for determining where the path of progress is headed:

PATH OF PROGRESS GUIDELINES

- **Guideline 1: Look for major retailers.** Companies like Best Buy, Lowe's, Costco, and Home Depot do not just build their stores on any spot. They do an exhaustive amount of research before they select a site, so you know they see potential in the area.
- **Guideline 2: Check to see where new highways are headed.** That tells you where properties will likely be available for development.
- **Guideline 3: Look for cities or neighborhoods where revitalization efforts are taking place.** Many times, cities with blighted areas form redevelopment districts and offer incentives to attract investors, providing you with an opportunity. However, be sure that the local leaders and agencies actually have a clear and definite plan for redevelopment, the revenues to back up that plan, and the political clout to carry through the plan.

You will be in competition with other investors who are also looking to determine where the path of progress is headed. It pays for you to do your homework to get in early. Our recommendation is to seek out properties that can be rezoned from residential to commercial. These are often overlooked by investors with a deep pool of resources available to them. Their eyes are on bigger prizes, allowing you to sneak in under the radar. To see if the rezoning climate is favorable, check with the appropriate governmental agency to determine whether similar rezoning requests have been granted. If this is the case, you are good to go on a rezoning campaign.

DEMOGRAPHICS

The term "demographics" refers to the makeup of the population within a given investment area; that is, number of families, earning power, mean age, and growth trends. When an area shows steady growth, there will be more demand for services and businesses to serve a larger population, opening up commercial investment opportunities for you. You can get demographic information from companies who specialize in it. The cost is not great, and it is well worth the investment. Below are the basic elements of demographics so you can get an idea of the information you will receive in such reports.

Job Growth/Levels of Income

In terms of future investments, you will obviously want good job growth in a targeted area. After all, good jobs bring more people into the area, and those people will need housing and services. As a starting point for your research, consider using the U.S. Bureau of Labor Statistics **http:// www.bls.gov/**. The BLS tracks job statistics on a national, state, and local level.

Diversity of Businesses

A diverse number of businesses and jobs is your protection against economic downturns. The general rule is the more diverse the economy, the less a recession will damage the commercial real estate market. An example is Detroit, which is so tightly tied to the automotive market that its economy bounces up and down in relation to car sales. Seattle is another example where the economy has been tied to the aircraft manufacturing market.

Types of Industries

Different industries have different growth rates. For example, the farming sector is traditionally slow-growing so real estate values will tend to grow slowly as well. At the other end of the spectrum, technology industries (computers, software) grow fast. This means that areas where they locate will cause property values to rise faster. Therefore, you know if you invest in a high-tech area, your income flow and price appreciation will be much greater.

Job Outsourcing

Job outsourcing can create havoc in a local economy. When jobs go overseas, businesses and plants close, creating a negative ripple effect. Unemployment rises, employees move elsewhere to seek jobs, and local businesses lose customers. In short, outsourcing can cause a downturn in the local economy and create poor investment environment. Therefore, analyze the data closely to make sure jobs will not be lost to overseas companies. A good indicator of a stable economy is companies' paying stable or increasing wages. They know there is a market for their goods or services, and they do not plan to move production out of the country.

Check for levels of unemployment as well. Obviously, you will want declining unemployment. Finally, seek out areas that include businesses and governmental agencies that are traditionally resistant to economic downturns (education, government, and medical services).

School Districts

You always want to invest in areas with excellent school systems because they are important to parents. School systems drive expansion, which is to your benefit as an investor. Beyond education, parents and their school-age children require a multitude of services, such as day-care centers, restaurants, and grocery stores which drive more growth — again, to your benefit. Our advice is to become acquainted with your local school board. Like highways, new schools take a long time to plan and build, and the school board should have valuable statistics available to the public. These statistics can help you plan your investment strategy in a sound manner.

THE LOCAL AREA

After checking out the demographic information listed above, zero in on local areas to make sure they have all the factors for success. Avoid declining, overbuilt areas. Avoid locales where properties are expensive or overpriced. In these spots, you can really do damage to your cash flow if you invest; plus there is little opportunity for appreciation that would make the investment worthwhile. Expensive properties can also be difficult to sell; therefore, look for properties between the two extremes. They are easier to buy, easier to sell, and demand is greater overall. You will also enjoy greater cash flow and appreciation.

The basic laws of supply and demand apply in your local area just as they do on the regional or national levels. Your aim: strong demand and limited supply. This situation creates shortages and opportunities for you. You can evaluate supply and demand through a number of indicators; for example, the following factors indicate that supply is greater than demand:

- Large number of building permits
- Weak absorption or rental of new properties
- Excess of income property listings

The result is low occupancy, low rents, and rental concessions. This situation ends up costing you in terms of lower cash flow and smaller appreciation potential. Of course, if you have the following indicators, you are in a good position to invest:

- Few vacancies
- Strong absorption or rental of new properties
- Few income property listings

Let us get specific in terms of the indicators you should examine to evaluate the investment worthiness of a local area.

Building Permits

Building permits are a clear indicator of future real estate supply. If there are too many over a long period of time, it may indicate oversupply of properties. Too few permits indicate that interest rates are too high or the market is saturated. In either case, you have to sort through these influences to make sure you have a good environment for investment.

Positive absorption means the demand for space is greater than the supply, and it is a good measure of the health of the real estate market. If available, new properties are rented within months, and there is a robust market. Absorption is measured differently in residential markets compared to commercial markets. Residential properties are measured in housing units while commercial properties are measured in square footage. Obviously, you want to avoid negative absorption markets in which real estate properties are in oversupply.

Your local planning or building departments can supply information on building permits. Absorption numbers are harder to come by, but you can get them from local real estate appraisers and brokers, especially brokers holding CCIM (Certified Commercial Investment Member) certification. They specialize in the sale of income properties and normally track absorption statistics.

Keep in mind that both building permits and absorption are specific to different types of properties. This means one type of property, industrial for example, will not have an influence on other types, such as commercial or retail, unless the use of a property is changed.

Access

Access is vitally important to any commercial property. Any property with ease of access will have a higher value than one with difficult access. In particular, retail businesses depend on customer traffic. Another factor in access is the government body with responsibility for the roads fronting commercial properties. You may have to petition them to create access to vacant tracts of land. For example, assume you have raw land and want to build a strip mall on it. The first questions you will need to ask yourself are, "Can I get a permit to install curb cuts and entrance/exit lanes so there is easy access to the highway? Where can I install them? How many can I install?"

Traffic Count

State departments of transportation and city highway departments keep traffic counts that are available to the public free or at a low cost. To get the information, simply contact the appropriate department. You may want to ask for a historical record of the area you are considering to learn past trends. Obviously, a long-term decline in traffic may determine that it is being siphoned off by newer highways elsewhere and may indicate a poor climate for investment, depending on the type. An increase in traffic may indicate potential for future investment. The good news is that, under normal circumstances, new highways take a long time to plan and build. That means you can keep an eye on the progress of the project and plan your investments accordingly.

Traffic Flow

Simply put, traffic flow refers to which way traffic moves on a street or highway and at what time of day. Morning and evening have the greatest number of vehicles on the road. You can study the flow to find out how many drivers are local or distant residents. From that, you can extrapolate how many will patronize local businesses on a regular basis. For example, if a strong local traffic flow is indicated, you know it is likely that your business tenants will get a greater number of those customers than they would get from customers located farther away. This, in turn, indicates the type of tenants you need in your properties.

Plats

A plat is a recorded and approved survey of a tract of land. The tract can be a single parcel of land or entire subdivision. The purpose of the platting process is to ensure that all comply with specified standards for development. Broadly speaking, this process is intended to protect the public's health, safety, and welfare. More specifically, it keeps legal ownership of land clear and helps prevents disputes among property buyers. The information in a plat survey varies according to city, county, or state regulations. Usually it contains the following information:

- **A legal description.** Usually, a plat is given a simple description like "Mandan Plat #2" or a "second replat of Abrasives, Inc., a total of 52.03 acres and zone change from "A" Agricultural to "IA" Industrial. Located in Section 27 and 28, Township 139 North, Range 88 West." Plats are determined by the local governing body, usually a county commission or city council.

- **Dimensions of the property.** All dimensions (length, width) will be shown.

- **Plat items.** Easements for roads and utilities, roadways, and other elements, such as ponds.

- **Plat notes.** Often, these notes concern restrictions agreed on between the governing body and the owner at the time of approval. Restrictions may refer to such items as maximum square footage of a building, a defined use of the property, and other limitations. Pay close attention to the plat notes. If you want a property for a specific use, buy it, and then find out the plat notes forbid that use, you will end up with a useless investment unless you can convince the governing body to rewrite its restrictions.

- **Plat date.** You should also pay close attention to the date for this reason: A property seller may offer you a plat that has a vacant plot on which you would like to build an office building, and the record may show it is zoned for such a project. However, that same seller may have had the property replatted in the previous year to accommodate a tenant who wanted to build a strip mall. When you check the plat notes, you find that the target property has a new use, one that does not include building an office building. If you had not checked the date and the notes, you would have been stuck with property unusable for your investment intentions.

Since such problems can arise, it is best to prevent them by checking and double-checking plat records to make sure they fit the zoning requirements and your intended use. You can protect yourself in two ways. First, add a provision to your purchase agreement that specifies a review of plat information is part of your due diligence period and that the seller will cooperate in providing those documents to you. Second, hire an experienced real estate lawyer to review the documents for you. His or her advice can save you a lot of heartache and expense.

ZONING

Properties are zoned for specific uses: residential, commercial, office, and industrial. Therefore, you should pay close attention to zoning regulations and ordinances because they can dramatically affect your investment in positive or negative ways. For example, *use of property* is a vital element of zoning. Assume you want to build a strip mall that will include a restaurant. Any restaurant owner wants ample parking space for customers. The first question you have to ask yourself is this: Do local codes allow you to include enough parking spaces? The answer may vary according to the code. If the answer is no, you will have to seek permission or change plans. You can head this problem off by performing due diligence up front. You need site plan approval from the local planning authority. If you do not get approval, you need to go back to that authority and request a variance, which can be expensive and time consuming. Protect yourself every step of the way, from the initial building application to the final steps of the project.

Another important principle is to remember to *use governs value*. For example, if you buy or option vacant land and get it fully prepared, you can then sell it to developers seeking that kind of property. Therefore, if you have vacant property zoned for commercial/retail use and developers want to build a hotel or restaurant on it, you can expect a good profit because you had the foresight to tie up that property.

Another important principle in relation to use is *rezoning*. For example, you know the local governing bodies favor economic growth, and you have a residential or industrial property that can be rezoned for commercial use. Knowing this, you can approach the governing body and ask to rezone the property. Once rezoning is accomplished, the property value will jump, all other things being equal, and you can earn a profit.

A final principle is a reminder: Real estate laws vary from community to community. If you invest in one area and want to invest in another, do not make the mistake of assuming that the laws are the same. Local ordinances can be different, vague, and confusing because different governing bodies interpret codes and regulations differently. If this is the case, you will need to seek clarification from the appropriate official. Be sure to get that clarification in writing. Beyond that, if you still find the written clarification vague, go to the city attorney and get a legal opinion on the exact meaning of the language.

A WORD ON POLITICS

Different communities approach development in different ways. Some are highly pro-development; others are anti-development. Then there is the in-between: Both forces are present and in conflict with each other. If the local economy needs a boost, it is likely that the pro-development forces will be in the ascendance, and your job will be easier. However, if anti-development forces predominate, you will have a decision to make: foregoing development or working to convince everyone involved that your development will be an asset to the overall health of the community. It helps to be an excellent communicator, so if you are not presently a polished speaker and presenter, it would definitely be to your benefit to acquire those skills.

CHAPTER 5

THE SWEETEST ASPECT OF COMMERCIAL REAL ESTATE INVESTMENT — VALUE

In the introduction to this book, we briefly covered the concept of value in commercial real estate investment. This chapter will explore that concept more deeply because it is one of the most important reasons for investing. Real estate value has several components that you need to understand thoroughly to make maximum impact with your investments.

OTHER PEOPLE'S MONEY (OPM)

This is a standard concept that underpins any kind of real estate investment — commercial, residential, industrial, and so on. Simply put, it is money you borrow to get into the game. This money can come from institutional lenders (banks, credit unions, S&L pension funds) private lenders, or any number of sources. In terms of commercial real estate, financing may sound complicated, but it all boils down to this:

- You borrow money from a lender to buy a property.

- You receive income from tenants in that property.

- You pay back the lender with tenant income.

- Eventually, you pay back the loan and receive profit from your property.

OPM allows you to make use of an important tool in commercial real estate investment — leverage.

LEVERAGE

As stated above, using other people's money allows you to get into the market by investing a minimum of your own capital. To get leverage, you need to get that money at a lower cost than the return you get on your investments. Here is an example to illustrate how leverage works: Assume you bought a property for $100,000 with a down payment of 20 percent ($20,000). To complete the transaction, you need to borrow $80,000 ("80 percent loan-to-value"). If you wanted to, you could sell that property for, say, $120,000. The result is a gross profit of $20,000 or a 20 percent rate of return (ROR). But you have actually accomplished more through leverage. You used the leverage of the $80,000 loan to increase the rate of return from 20 percent on the property's gross price to a 100 percent rate of return on the $20,000 down payment. Plus, without leverage, you would have needed $100,000 to buy the property, a sum that is not within the range of ordinary people.

EQUITY

Another important component of value is the build up of equity. Assuming you keep an investment property in good shape with good tenants, you should be able to increase rents over time. So, once you pay off the $80,000 loan (using tenant money) mentioned above, you have an equity build up of $80,000 — even if the property value did not go up (an unlikely event).

APPRECIATION

Hand in hand with equity build up comes appreciation — the increase in value of a property over time. And most real estate properties tend to do just that — increase in value. One factor influencing appreciation is that inflation tends to drive up the replacement cost of properties. Another is the law of supply and demand. That is, as the population increases, so does the demand for ownership. In modern times, real estate has consistently increased in value at a rate of about 6.1 percent on a yearly basis. This can be considered "passive" appreciation; that is, you do not need to do anything to receive this benefit. Beyond that, however, you can enjoy the benefits of "active" appreciation. That is, you can actively undertake actions to increase the value of a property. For example, as a forward-looking investor, you may be considering a property zoned for an office building. At the present moment, it faces a residentially-zoned area across the street. But, from your study of the area, you know the trend is for the neighborhood to become busier and noisier over the years (perhaps because of the construction of a new highway nearby). So, it is possible that residential housing will decline due to increased traffic and noise, increasing the likelihood that zoning laws will shift to a broader use. By buying the commercial property (or building on it), you enjoy the opportunity to gain a future of higher appreciation and rate of return on that property. 59

INCOME

Commercial real estate properties can provide a good source of steady income (assuming you manage the properties well). For example, in a professional office building, you will have many tenants paying you rent. So, unlike residential single-family homes, it is highly unlikely that you will ever have a 100 percent vacancy rate. Someone will always be providing a source of income for you. With astute management, you can keep your vacancy rate low and your income high.

PEACE OF MIND

With commercial real estate investment, you can create security for yourself and your family. You are not tied to a corporation or a boss who can downsize you in the blink of an eye. Instead, you are your own boss and create your own future. All of the benefits mentioned above — OPM, leverage, appreciation, and income — lead to wealth and a secure future.

CHAPTER 6

UNDERSTANDING REAL ESTATE MARKET PSYCHOLOGY & VALUE

One day the stock market rises, only to fall the next. But what drives this movement? Despite all the technical analysis that experts spout, the basis of the movement is two very human emotions — fear and greed. Investors fear they will lose money and sell stocks or they see an opportunity to rake in the bucks. We do not mean that every investor is greedy or fearful. It is just that these emotions tend to drive the stock market. After all, no one wants to lose money, and everyone wants to make money.

Fear and greed drive the real estate market, but there is one other emotion involved — pride. By this, we mean pride of ownership. Every person who owns a home or other property has pride in it. We bring pride up because it is an emotion that will need to be dealt with, particularly with residential properties. Because of pride of ownership, homeowners will tend to overvalue their homes in negotiations. Investors cannot get caught up in their emotions. Remain objective and decide on the value based on a market analysis. Be sure to get a lease option on a house at a wholesale price, not a retail one. Otherwise, a profit will not be made. So make a low offer. If the seller takes the offer, fine. If he or she insists on a retail price, move on. The deal is not right then.

Let us now take a closer look at the primary values every real estate investor uses to evaluate potential investments.

UNIVERSAL DETERMINANTS OF VALUE

In any real estate market, there are four essential factors that determine the value of properties:

- **Demand** — The more people want a property, the higher the price goes.

- **Scarcity** — This is the supply/demand ratio. When properties are scarce, prices go up; when there is an oversupply, prices go down.

- **Transferability** — A clear title is absolutely essential to lease options or any other form of real estate transaction. If there is no clear title to a property, it is essentially worthless because it will end up in a time- and money-consuming legal entanglement at best or no sale at worst.

- **Utility** — The more uses a property has, the more potential it has for profit simply because there are so many more ways to sell it or the lease option.

In the previous chapter, we discussed the general forces that influence value — economics, physical forces, political, and social. Now let us get deeper into the subject by looking at specific factors that influence value.

SPECIFIC DETERMINANTS OF VALUE

The determinants listed below are ones that investors need to be very familiar with. They will guide decisions on whether or not to purchase a lease option.

- **Appraised value** — Value an appraiser places on a piece of real estate; the figure is usually at or near retail value.

- **Loan value** — Value a lender places on a piece of real estate; this figure often varies as a percentage of the appraised value.

- **Property tax value** — Value tax assessor places on a piece of real estate; the figure could be higher or lower than the retail value.

- **Replacement value** — Value insurance companies place on the improvements on a piece of real estate; the figure is determined by a cost approach.

- **Retail value** — The value an owner or end-user places on a piece of real estate; this tends to be the highest value because of the pride of ownership factor mentioned earlier.

- **Wholesale value** — The value investors place on a piece of real estate; this tends to be the lowest value.

Once these six values are understood, the value of a specific property can be determined.

THREE METHODS OF VALUATION

There are three widely accepted approaches to determining the fair market value of a property: the cost approach, the sales comparison approach, and the income approach. Real estate appraisers will use one or more of these methods to determine the value of a property.

The Cost Approach

Basically, the cost approach method values two elements of a property — the land and the improvements on the land. It then determines the accrued depreciation of the improvements. This is then subtracted from the total value to arrive at the property value. Below is an example of how it works. An accrued depreciation of $50,000 is assumed.

Land Value	$ 150,000
Improvements	+ $ 350,000
Total	$ 500,000
Accrued Depreciation	- $ 50,000
Property Value	$ 450,000

Generally speaking, the cost approach method is most reliable when used on newer structures, but it tends to become less reliable as properties grow older.

The Income Approach

This method analyzes the income a property produces in order to determine its value. The more income a property produces, the higher its value. Income can be figured in two ways. The first is the gross rent multiplier method. The formula looks like this:

Value = Gross Annual Rent x Gross Rent Multiplier (GRM)

Call a commercial real estate company or other source in the area to find out what the gross rent multiplier is. In the example below, we assume the gross annual rent is $150,000, and the GRM for the area is 7.

Gross Rent	$ 150,000
GRM	x 7
Property Value	$1,050,000

The second method to use is called the income capitalization approach and is a little more complicated. The formula looks like this:

Value = Income ÷ Capitalization Rate

In this method, the income is the net operating income (NOI). NOI is the gross income of the property minus the operating expenses. The market in which the property is located determines the capitalization rate.

Again, this rate can be found by calling a commercial real estate company in the city and asking for the figure. Here is how the method works: Assume an investor is looking at a property and the NOI is $70,000 with a capitalization rate of 7 percent. The property value would be determined this way:

NOI	$ 70,000
Capitalization Rate	÷ .07
Property Value	$1,000,000

If the capitalization rate for the same property was 8 percent, then the value would be lower at $875,000.

The Sales (Market) Comparison Approach

The comps method looks at the price or price per unit area of similar properties being sold in the marketplace. One property is compared to similar properties to determine value in terms of age, condition, amenities, time of sale, size, location, etc. Prices are then adjusted to account for differences. Let us use a single-family home example to illustrate this practice.

Assume an investor wants to know the value of a 1,500 square foot home with two bedroom, two baths, and an attached two-car garage. To find the comparable value, check similar properties that have sold within the past six months in the same neighborhood. For purposes of this exercise, we will assume there are two comparable properties. The first comparable property is 1,500 square feet, has two bedrooms, two baths, and an attached two-car garage. It sold for $180,000 30 days ago. The second comparable home is 1,600 square feet, has three bedrooms, two bathrooms, and an attached two-car garage. It sold for $200,000 45 days ago. Calculate the cost per square foot for each of the properties by dividing the sale price by the square footage. Here are the results: The first comparable property has a cost per square foot of $120 (180,000 ÷ 1,500). The second has a cost per square foot of $125 (200,000 ÷ 1,600). To estimate the value of the target home, take the lower square footage figure of the first comparable property and multiply by the square footage of the target home. The result is:

$$1,500 \text{ sq. feet}$$
$$\underline{x \qquad \$120}$$
$$\text{Value} = \$180,000$$

Of course, this is a preliminary figure. Do a walk-through of the property to determine its actual condition. We will consider walk-through evaluations in more detail in Chapter 10.

Be aware that there are different types of comparables and methods of recognizing value in the area(s) being targeted:

- **Appreciation rates** — These indicate the annual percentage increases in the market value of properties. They will provide an indication of how hot or cold the market is. Doubt-digit appreciation rates say the market is hot, while single-digit rates indicate it is good. A cold real estate market is shown in zero or negative rates.

- **Sold comparables** — This is the first method to determine value as shown in our example above. Basically, sold comparables set the base for the retail value of real estate. This category of comparables is useful for properties sold within the past six months. Any property sold beyond the six month time period is not considered a good comparable.

- **Listing comparables** — These are properties currently on the market which are similar to the target property. This category sets the upper limit for the retail value of real estate because they have not sold or closed escrow. They simply indicate what sellers would like to get for their properties.

- **Expired comparables** — These are properties that have never sold nor closed escrow. They show the value beyond the present market in terms of what buyers are willing to pay. Generally speaking, retail buyers will buy the lower-priced comparable properties.

- **Pending comparables** — These are properties that have sold, but not closed escrow. They show the direction of value. When a pending comparable closes escrow, it then becomes a sold comparable. For example, if sold comparables are indicating a value of $150,000 and the pending comparables are showing a value of $158,000, then it indicates the value trend is headed upward.

- **New or planned developments** — As discussed earlier, this is the path of progress and serves as an indicator that properties in the path will appreciate in value.

- **Vacancies** — High vacancy rates may indicate problems with the property and/or neighborhood. Low vacancy rates indicate potentially profitable properties.

SOURCES OF FINANCING

Beginners in lease options will need to learn about and become an expert on sources of financing for lease options. Here is a brief summary of possible sources and the advantages and disadvantages of each:

Conventional Financing

This is the traditional approach to buying property. It is taken by qualifying for a new loan from a bank or mortgage lender. In most cases, there is a minimum 10 percent down payment plus closing costs. Many people take this route because it provides the ability to purchase almost any property with a good interest rate. The disadvantage is that only so many of these loans can be qualified for. Banks and mortgage lenders are conservative by nature and they'll balk if a person attempts to take out too many of these loans, particularly with single-family properties.

Fixed-Rate Unsecured Lines of Credit

These lines are issued through unsecured credit cards. If this route is chosen, seek out ones with fixed-rate and low interest. An unsecured loan is made solely on the promise to repay. The lender will need to consider the investor a good risk. The best way to be considered a good risk is to have no debt and a very high credit score (in the top 5 to 10 percent). The advantage of an unsecured line of credit is that, unlike a home equity loan, a person's house does not have to be put up as collateral and expensive closing costs charged by lenders don't have to be paid. One disadvantage is that, unless a person has zero debt and a high credit score, higher interest rates will likely be paid — defeating the purpose of getting such a line of credit in the first place. A second disadvantage is the temptation to over-borrow and accumulate debt that is not needed.

Home Equity Loans

There are two types of home equity loans — closed-end and line of credit. A closed-end loan is similar to a home mortgage; that is, a specific amount of money is loaned out and scheduled monthly repayments of principal and interest must be made. Another way to look at a closed-end loan is as a second mortgage. The date by which the loan must be repaid is set when the money is borrowed. Often interest rates are fixed.

To obtain financing for lease options, choose the second type — a home equity line of credit. This option acts more like a credit card and allows a person to use as much or as little of the credit line as desired, up to an approved dollar amount. It has the advantage of allowing a person to withdraw money when they want to use it. Normally, a person has between five and 20 years to access this credit line. Once the period has ended, borrowing must be stopped and the principal and interest must be repaid.

A typical range of repayment is between ten and 20 years. Or there may be balloon payments, which require the principal to be paid in one lump payment. Often, the credit interest rate is adjustable; that means the rate changes as the economy fluctuates. In general, home equity loans have several advantages. The rates tend to be lower than credit card rates or consumer loans. Such loans are also flexible. They allow a person to choose when to use the money. In addition, a person may be able to decide when to repay the principle. Another advantage is tax-deductibility. The interest paid is tax deductible up to $100,000 or the equity value in the home, whichever is less. Check with tax professional for details on the subject.

Home equity loans also have disadvantages. There is a risk of losing one's home if the loan cannot be repaid or refinanced. That is because the home is collateral for the money being borrowed and is subject to foreclosure. Being late or missing loan payments can trigger foreclosure within 60 to 90 days. In that case, a person will be forced to sell or lose the home.

Another disadvantage is the possibility of rising interest rates. If there is a variable rate, the monthly payments can rise or fall, depending on the economy. Most variable interest loans have "caps;" a cap sets how high the interest rate can increase each year as well as how much it can increase over the whole loan time period. Be sure to know what the cap is on the loan's interest rate. Finally, there are fees with home equity loans — origination fees application fees, withdrawal fees, etc. Be sure to find out what fees are being charged up front so unnecessary expenses can be avoided.

Private Financing

Private financing can be found through an arrangement with investment partners. Generally speaking, this is not a strategy for beginners simply because they do not have the track record to impress potential investors. However, it is definitely a goal to aim for due to its advantages in buying lease options and property in general. First, due to the cumulate wealth of the investors, larger equity positions and can be acquired and thus properties that are potentially much more profitable. Second, the hassle of qualifying for loans from conventional lenders is eliminated. Third, closings are much less expensive, much easier, and definitely much quicker. Fourth, funds from retirement accounts can be accessed to buy investment property. Fifth, those who invest money from such accounts can typically get much higher returns than in certificates of deposit or money-market funds. Finally, foreign investors cannot easily qualify for loans in the United States so private financing gives them access to the market — and provides an additional source of funds.

Seller Financing

This occurs when the original owner of a property wants the investor to step in to help them. For example, if pre-foreclosure is in the works, they will want someone to take over the financing and the property and pay the arrears. This approach has several advantages. First, a new loan is not being obtained; the current loan is just being taken over and payments are being made. That means no loan fees or down payments. Second, time is saved since a new loan does not need to be applied for. Instead, the closing is relatively quick and cheap. The disadvantage of this approach is that many sellers will not agree to it. Seller financing is not as open a route as other methods.

Information Sources

The Internet is a wonderful source for information on both residential and commercial properties. Use data from the sources listed below to get a good and realistic idea of the value of properties being considered. Be sure to make use of them. Both the residential and commercial sources listed below are among the most prominent, but other sources can be found.

ONLINE SOURCES FOR RESIDENTIAL PROPERTIES

- DataQuick — **dataquick.com**
- Domania — **domania.com**
- HomeGain — **homegain.com**
- HomeRadar.com — **homeradar.com**

ONLINE SOURCES FOR COMMERCIAL PROPERTIES

- CoStar Commercial — **costar.com**
- DataQuick — **dataquick.com**
- Intelius — **intelius.com**
- LoopNet — **loopnet.com**
- IDM Corporation — **idmdata-now.com**
- National Real Estate Index — **graglobal.com**
- REIS Inc. — **reis.com**

CHAPTER 7

THE PLAYERS IN THE COMMERCIAL REAL ESTATE INVESTMENT GAME

Commercial real estate investment is not an individual sport; it is a team sport. While you may be an individual investor, you can get nothing done without the help of other professionals. That is why it is important to understand the roles of the other players in the game and how you can make maximum use of their talents and experience. This chapter will provide you with that information.

REAL ESTATE INVESTMENT BROKERS

These are the "middlemen" through whom you buy, manage, and sell properties. For example, it is likely you will buy undeveloped land through a raw land broker. Once you have the property under control, you will use the services of a leasing agent, also known as a broker. At the other end, when you decide to sell a property, you will use the services of an investment broker. As you can tell from these "divisions of labor," brokers tend to specialize in specific areas. Their fees vary with the specialty. Raw land brokers charge commissions in the range of 6 to 10 percent. The investment broker charges from 1 to 3 percent for a transaction. The fee is smaller, but the transactions are larger. The leasing agent's fee is figured on a lease-by-lease basis and will vary according to rental rate, lease type, and lease terms. It will pay for you to have good relations with each of these individuals, especially if you plan to make commercial real estate investment a long-term career.

ARCHITECTS AND ENGINEERS

You will need the services of these professionals when you get involved in the construction of buildings on your investment properties or when you need to alter an existing building. In the latter case, you will need the advice and guidance of "space planners," architects who deal with the interior of a building to improve it for new or existing tenants. If you construct a building from scratch, you will need the services of several professionals:

- A surveyor, who draws up a boundary survey and a topographic map.

- A civil engineer, who designs the foundations and site improvements.

- A structural engineer, who designs the structure of the building.

- An architect, who designs the building exterior and the components of the building and acts as coordinator for all the other professionals.

There are various ways to use the services of these individuals. Those investors who like to keep things simple hire the architect to be responsible for all aspects of the project. This arrangement is the most expensive. Other investors like to take a more hands-on approach. They hire the architect and then hire the other professionals directly. This approach has the advantage of being less costly, and it helps you keep control of a project. It also increases your knowledge of the building process which, over the long haul, can help you keep costs down while improving the quality of your buildings. The disadvantage of this method is that it is time consuming. One approach to take is to involve yourself in the building process early in your career and, as your business grows, delegate this responsibility to a trusted associate. Doing so means you can concentrate on the large picture of building your investment portfolio and a secure financial future.

REAL ESTATE ATTORNEYS

It pays to have an experienced real estate lawyer available for your projects. Look for one who is experienced and specializes in your particular kind of investments. The attorney's function is to protect your interests at every step. Payment will vary with the project and your needs. From your point of view as an investor, a flat fee is best. However, there are instances when you might want the attorney to put money into a project. This self-interest guarantees that the attorney will be paying close attention to all legal aspects of the investment.

Attorneys are necessary to commercial real estate

investments because there are so many legal documents involved. In alphabetical order, the most common documents are:

- Architect's contract

- Brokerage agreement (leases)

- Building lease

- Easement documents

- Engineering contracts (civil, structural, surveys, testing)

- Entitlement and application forms

- Estoppel agreements

- Loan documents

- Ownership document (partnership, corporation, LLC)

- Property documents (operating agreements, reciprocal easements)

- Property management agreements (including subcontracts)

- Purchase agreements

- Title report

- Utility agreement

Your lawyer should be well-versed in every aspect of those documents to make sure they are all legally enforceable and hold the stated parties accountable for their responsibilities and actions. Remember, proper documentation is everything, not only in terms of making sure the project is done right and on time, but also in terms of your return on investment and capital gains. You will also need the services of an attorney for any existing building property you own because you will require legal documents specific to this investment, including:

- Existing leases

- Estoppel agreements

- Exclusive leasing or listing agreements

- New lease

- New/old loan documents

- Operating agreements

- Ownership documents

- Property management documents

- Purchase agreement

- Sales agreement

- Title documents

These are the most common documents; you may find that more are required for specific transactions.

CONTRACTORS

Contractors are the builders on a project. They do the actual raising of the physical structure, if building from scratch, or remodeling of an existing building. If you are building from the ground up, it makes sense to have an experienced, well-financed construction company on the job. If you are buying an existing property, you can use a smaller company. Often, construction companies specialize so you can hire several contractors to do different jobs. A large company will build the exterior structure while another completes interior work. In terms of an existing building, you can hire a company that specializes in tenant improvement.

You will want to negotiate contracts with each of these companies to make sure the project is on time and within budget. In terms of your investment, you need the building to be of the highest quality possible within the limits of the budget. Be sure to include a design review process as part of the contract; otherwise, cost overruns can kill you. Warranties can help you maintain discipline with contractors. When working with tenant improvement contractors, you need to negotiate a budget with the tenants and then monitor contractors closely to ensure they stay within the budget.

When you buy an existing investment property, you should know its condition at the time of the sale. As part of due diligence, seek to include the tenant improvement contractor in the process of inspecting the building. That way, the contractor will have a baseline knowledge of the improvements needed and can project costs more accurately, saving you time and money. A professional contractor interested in a long-term relationship with you will be able to suggest ways to keep maintenance costs at a minimum.

PROPERTY MANAGERS

A good property manager is vital, particularly when

you buy an existing property. We do not recommend that you become a property manager yourself. You are an entrepreneur and are taking calculated risks, as every entrepreneur should. You think big picture. Property managers have an entirely different skill set and outlook. They should be conservative and concerned with keeping tenants happy, while keeping costs under control. They collect rents and enforce leases. They should protect your investment and be skilled at handling the inevitable conflicts that arise with tenants. A good property manager will keep conflicts to a minimum, only calling you in when no other resolution is possible.

We recommend that you bring in an experienced property manager in the beginning of a project to examine the architect or contractor's plans to make sure that the beauty of design does not interfere with the everyday management of a building. After all, architects do not have to deal with water leaks, frost and freeze expansion and contraction, heating and cooling defects. The classic example is the famed architect, Frank Lloyd Wright, and the design of the Johnson's Wax building that leaked like a sieve until rubber gaskets were installed between the roof and the supports. A good property manager will help you make sure the architect's dream meshes with the reality of a properly constructed building.

An experienced property manager is also vital to the management of an existing building. He or she can examine such a building from a structural point of view and also closely scrutinize the current rent roll and expenses. Such examinations can identify cost-saving areas and troublesome tenants. An experienced property manager should be one of your primary investments in constructing a new building or the management and maintenance of existing structures.

You can see that an experienced and professional team is central to your investment success, but you should always be head of that team and the final decision-maker because it is your money and your future.

CHAPTER 8

SOURCES OF INFORMATION ON COMMERCIAL REAL ESTATE PROPERTIES

There are multiple sources of information on commercial real estate properties, and you should use a mix of them. This chapter will outline several sources. We recommend that you try them out and then select the ones that work best in your area and for your individual style.

DIRECT CONTACTS

Direct contact with owners, brokers, and tenants is often the best method of finding properties and deals. Think of contact as an opportunity to hone your people skills and break the ice with people who can help your career. After all, you have to make yourself known to get into the game. If you are already in the business in some capacity, such as a leasing agent, this is even better for you. You can contact potential customers and let them know you are getting started in commercial real estate investments. A good idea is to contact people in your specialty. Do not take a shotgun approach and seek contacts in all the specialties at once. You will spread your resources too thin and end up accomplishing little.

COLD CALLS

If you dislike cold calls, it is a good idea to get past this attitude quickly. There is no denying that they can be effective as long as you approach contacts in a professional and courteous manner, and as long as they can see some benefit in talking with you. Time is money to investors and clients, and they do not appreciate its being wasted. When you make a cold call, have a definite purpose and benefits in mind. Use the "elevator pitch" approach whether making a cold call via telephone or in person: Explain your proposal in the time it takes an elevator to move from one floor to another, or about one minute. To refine your approach, practice it ahead of time. Make five cold calls a day, every day. Consistent practice will get you past a negative attitude, especially when you discover it brings in profitable business.

BUSINESS AND PROFESSIONAL ORGANIZATIONS

Such organizations are an excellent source of contacts and provide you with the opportunity to integrate yourself into the local business community. It will help for you to join the local Chamber of Commerce, civic groups, and a local real estate organization. If you want to refine your speaking skills, join Toastmasters and gain valuable experience while making contacts. It never hurts to give back to your community, either, in the form of fund-raisers, United

Way, or other charitable pursuits. It is a win-win situation when you do so. The community receives help, and you build your reputation as a civic-minded individual. Do not limit your memberships to local organizations. Also join state, national, and international organizations that represent your specialty. For example, if you have targeted the shopping mall market, you could join the International Council of Shopping Centers **http://www.icsc.org/**. If your target area is the office or industrial market, you could join the Society of Industrial and Office Realtors **http://www. sior.com/**. Such organizations can be a valuable source of information and word of mouth referrals.

ADVERTISING

Advertising is a great way to reach a large audience at low cost. Newspaper ads, Internet ads, Yellow Page ads, and brochures allow you to spread the message about your services. Make sure all advertising projects the image you want to present to the world and is integrated to make sure your "branding" is consistent. The "brand" should be consistent with your target market and all the players in that market. For example, if you deal in farmland, you may want to project a down-to-earth image that is in sync with rural investors. On the other hand, if you are dealing in the office market, you will want to project a serious, sophisticated "white collar" image. If you are a natural "ham" and like to appear in front of people, you can give speeches or create and present seminars on the subject of commercial real estate investment, assuming you are experienced in the field. They can be put on free or at low cost, and you can gather leads as a result.

NEWSPAPER ARTICLES

Always make it a point to keep up to date through the business section of your local newspaper. Articles can keep you abreast of what is happening in the community and can indicate future trends in terms of development and expansion.

PUBLIC RECORDS

Your local city and county government offices have public tax rolls, lists of property owners that you can examine in person or online. Title offices also have lists of property owners that you can use to find likely prospects to contact.

FRIENDS AND ACQUAINTANCES

It never hurts to let friends, acquaintances, and neighbors know that you are in the market for properties. They may know someone who would like to do business with you. Sometimes, a casual conversation can yield great results.

LISTINGS

Once you have listings, keep a record of all prospects that call about those listings and try to build relationships with them, even if they are not currently in the market for what you are offering. They may want to buy from you in the future.

DRIVE-AROUNDS

This is a time-intensive method, but it keeps you in touch with what is happening in your area. Drive around and write a list of companies that might be prospects for your business. Once you have done that, you can contact them to see what investment possibilities exist.

TICKLER FILE

From the start of your investment career, keep a tickler file. This is an organizational method in which 12 folders represent months and 31 folders represent each day. You arrange them to remind yourself of activities to be done each day. On a particular day, you open the numbered folder representing that date and take all the items out of the folder and put the empty folder into the next month. It is an excellent way to keep on top of things like prospects, options, and expiration dates.

BROKERS, BANKS, AND OTHER FINANCIAL ORGANIZATIONS

All these institutions will have information on commercial real estate properties. Work to establish close relationships with all these organizations so you will be in a position to receive referrals from them.

WORD OF MOUTH

Once you establish yourself as an honest, reliable, successful investor, you will find that your reputation will bring business through the door. Everyone wants to deal with someone they can trust who makes them money. Work hard to establish a good reputation in your community.

OTHERS

Do not forget that anyone you deal with is a potential source of leads for more business. When you deal fairly and honestly with architects, contractors, attorneys, property managers, and engineers, they will spread the word. Of course, you can do the same for them. Work to build good relationships with all these individuals. It makes for a great working environment and spreads success around for everyone.

CHAPTER 9

FINDING PROFITABLE DEALS

Investors in commercial real estate deals have one purpose — to find undervalued properties that will turn a profit. To find these deals, be persistent. Undervalued properties do not just walk in the door. They are often below the radar. This chapter outlines several approaches that can be taken to locate these properties. Try any or all of them and keep the ones that work best.

Advertisements

Search for likely prospects in the newspaper, online, or in local real estate publications. Or place ads to gain prospects. Make the ads short, sweet, and immediately readable. Do not start throwing in abbreviations. Readers do not always know what the abbreviations mean and often get annoyed at having to decode them.

We recommend trying different styles of ads to see which ones draw the biggest and best responses. Beyond newspaper and Internet ads, do not forget publications like school directories, church fliers, etc. For a small price, these types of ads can support good causes and receive good exposure.

Bird Dogs

"Bird dogs" or "scouts" can be a good source of inside information. Essentially, these individuals have a single goal — to find potential deals and then sell that information to other investors. They charge a fee for this service and the fees vary. It all depends upon the property price and its profit potential. A bird dog may make from $250 to $1,000 on each lead that ends with a purchase by another investor. Becoming a professional bird dog is a great way to get started in the real estate market because it does not require any cash on a bird dog's part or any previous knowledge in order to look at properties. It is also the fastest way for them to earn cash. The main requirements for becoming a bird dog are time, motivation, and the patience to do lots of searching. They will use a combination of the following search techniques to find properties:

- Post flyers at grocery stores, laundromats, or other locations with lots of foot traffic and high visibility.

- Check the newspaper real estate section for such ads as "Handyman Special," "Fixer Upper," etc.

- Advertise in the local newspapers and online. Or they run their own ads in the Real Estate Wanted section of the newspaper.

- Drive around and note houses in disrepair or properties that have become obsolescent.

- Some get jobs as property inspectors. This way, they get a good sense of the market and the properties that are available.

When working with a bird dog, make sure they know the

goals and concentrate on the properties being looked for. In terms of "bird dogging," another, probably cheaper, course can be taken. Build a network of part-time scouts; that is, individuals with full-time jobs who are looking for extra cash. This network could include virtually anyone: business associates, coworkers, delivery truck drivers, dentists, doctors, employees, friends, mail carriers, neighbors, repair men, taxi drivers, tenants, trash collectors, utility meter readers, etc.

Business Cards

Have cards readily available at all times and hand them out. The cards should say specifically that a person buys or leases homes. Make sure that the contact information is printed on the cards: name, address, phone number, e-mail, Web site.

Chamber of Commerce

The local chamber should have a list of businesses coming into or leaving town so it can be a good source of current information.

Corporate Relocation Departments

These departments often have an inventory of properties that have not sold. If there is no company corporate buyout policy, the property owners would likely love a lease option. After all, they have already relocated and do not need the added burden of making payments on two homes.

Direct Mail

Done properly, direct mail is an inexpensive and easy way to contact out-of-town and problem property owners in the area. All that is needed is a computer application that has mail merge capabilities (Microsoft Word, WordPerfect, etc.) In the application, create a form letter which can then be merged with the appropriate names and addresses. Direct mail is also quick. Response will be received within two weeks' time. Plus, there are no third-party hassles. In the letters, keep the offer simple, direct, and clear.

Finder's Fees

Let people know that a finder's fee will be paid if they locate a property and the investor buys a lease option on it. Set the amount to pay, but it has to be attractive enough to entice people to locate properties. In his book, *How to Make Money with Real Estate Options*, Thomas J. Lucier says he pays $500.

Fliers

Post tear-off fliers in any prominent public place that allows them — drug stores, grocery stores, convenience shops, etc. They should have the same information as in the newspaper ads. Make them attractive so as to draw attention to them.

FSBOs

This term refers to "For Sale by Owner" postings. Often referred to as "fizz-bos," these are owners who attempt to sell their properties without the aid of a realtor. They often find it is much harder than they think it will be and get overwhelmed by the process of dealing with buyers, lenders, title companies, and other parties involved in the market. This hassle can motivate them to sell quickly. A timely letter or call from an investor can relieve them of aggravation and create a win-win situation for both parties.

Multiple Listing Services (MLS) — Long-Term Listings

Consider hiring a realtor to search listings that are over 90 to 120 days old. These properties are taking too long to sell and the owners will likely be motivated to deal.

Out-of-State Owners

Many out-of-state owners live far away from their properties and find it a burden to deal with the issues involving those properties. Perhaps they inherited the property or had to relocate. These individuals can be found by checking with the county's property tax roll. It should list the mailing address for the parcel. Contact the county property appraiser or assessor's office to see if they keep a database of property owners who reside outside the county. Or contact a private company, like those listed in the previous chapter, that maintains a similar database of real property ownership records.

Real Estate Investment Clubs

Such clubs are a prime opportunity to network with other investors so it is wise to join one. Often, they have unsold properties they want to sell or know of properties not in their area. Beyond that, investors can expand their knowledge of not only lease options, but other aspects of real estate that may be of interest. Remember that networking is a two-way street — be prepared to give as well as receive information.

Vacant Properties

A vacant home or other property says that someone is making payments on a property that is not being used. This can be a burden on the owner, but it is an opportunity for an investor to create a win-win situation by taking the property off their hands. Write the owner a letter. If there is no response, try the county tax rolls or the post office.

Word-of-Mouth

Once a reputation as a fair and honest investor has been established, leads and deals will come.

Three more categories — realtors, landlords, and qualified sellers — are extremely important and we have chosen to treat them at length as separate subjects in this chapter.

REALTORS

It is a fact that realtors control most of the real estate market in any city. That means they have access to sellers investors might like to target. It pays to work with realtors. They do not always like to work with investors, however, because it is harder to lowball a property and get the deal through — and realtors like deals because that is how they get their commissions. However, they will always have properties that do not sell or ones the seller feels the realtor is not selling fast enough. These are properties where creative solutions provided by investors can help them out.

Generally speaking, it is easier to approach realtors with lease option opportunities during a buyer's market because they do not get a commission if a property does not sell or if the listing expires and ends up listed with another realtor. Sellers also put more pressure on realtors to sell their homes in a buyer's market. This opens the door for investors because the realtor has to come up with alternative solutions in order to satisfy his or her customer. It is in an investor's best interest to educate realtors on the benefits of lease options and build solid business relationships with them.

The type of realtor to work with is called a *listing agent* — the agent who lists the property for the seller. Listing agents work with the property owners and try to build a reasonably close relationship with them in order to establish the trust that will result, eventually, in a sale and a commission. Because they do build these relationships, realtors find that owners tell them many things. Owners are not afraid to speak their minds when the property does not sell or does not sell quickly enough. Beyond sticking with the realtor or changing to a different one, their options often come down to two choices — taking the property off the market or renting it. These are two options the realtor does not want to hear. However, in their minds, the lesser of two evils is renting the property, and that is where the lease option investor comes into the picture. When the realtor gives an investor leads and he or she purchases the lease option, they know they will get a commission and get it paid quickly. That is because the investor will front the commission money (the seller always pays it as part of the transaction) for him or her. A win-win situation is created — the realtor sells the listing, the seller sells the property, and the investor buys an investment with lucrative potential.

Before any of this can be done, willing realtors must be found and relationships must be built with them. The first part is easy — listing agents are listed in the real estate section of the newspaper or online. Or they can be found through the investor groups mentioned earlier in this chapter. Also, once a good relationship is established with one realtor, he or she can provide access to other agents. The second part — building relationships — is harder but absolutely essential. It will take time so be committed and persistent. Investors need to convince brokers and realtors of the benefits of working with them and be able to answer the most basic of all business questions: What is in it for me?

After determining which properties have been listed for more than 90 days, employ these basic tactics:

Letters to Realtors

The letter should briefly mention the property the investor is interested in and quickly emphasize the benefits of considering a lease option and of dealing with an investor.

Phone Calls to Realtors

It is always best to follow up a letter with a phone call. In a realtor's busy day, letters can get lost or misplaced. A phone call also establishes a much more personal connection than a letter. Given a realtor's schedule, it is likely that message will have to be left on their answering service. This forces an investor to be succinct and get the benefits message across quickly. Also, if the realtor has no interest in the first place, it means valuable time has not be wasted in a longer phone call.

Presentations to Realtors

This is a cost-effective way of reaching several realtors at once in their office. To hold a presentation at the office, an invitation must be extended first. Such offices can be very busy places with many requests made to get on their meeting agendas. Cut through the clutter with a simple message: I can help you sell more of your listings. Ideally, the investor already has a contact within the real estate office that can assist in pushing the message through and get the investor on the agenda. If not, call directly and ask to speak to the broker or office manager. Introduce oneself, explain the purpose, and immediately emphasize the benefits of the lease option strategy. Tell them the presentation will be brief and not take up more than 10 to fifteen minutes of their time. The phone call can be preceded with a letter, letting the broker know to be expecting a phone call. This gives the investor the opportunity to not only list the benefits of the presentation, but also to provide references and testimonials from satisfied clients. An appointment may not be obtained the first time, but be persistent and contact the broker on a regular basis. During that time, he may have changed his mind or the market may have changed in the investor's favor.

In order to achieve the goal of establishing profitable relationships with realtors, educate them on lease options during the presentation. They may not be familiar with the concept simply because it was not part of their training. As part of gaining their real estate license, they learned about seller contracts, fair housing, legal issues, state and legal standards, etc., not creative options for making sales. Do not walk into a presentation assuming that every agent knows what lease options are. Be prepared to explain the concept in clear but not condescending language.

To be effective during a presentation, be thoroughly prepared ahead of time. This is no time to improvise. The best way to get organized is to prepare an agenda. This will keep thoughts in order and allow a powerfully effective case to be made in the allotted time. To ensure that the presentation receives a positive response right from the start be sure to take a simple step — bring bakery goods. It is expected in many offices.

Once the presentation has been made and questions have

been answered, it is likely that interested agents will offer leads. If not, it never hurts to ask in a polite way. Do not forget to follow up with realtors who have expressed interest. This is a crucial step. Real estate agents are very busy and talk to many people during the day. That is why they need polite reminders of the benefits an investor can provide them. Give them a call once a month or every other month, depending on their reaction to these calls. If business has not been done with a particular agent, simply say something similar to this:

> Hi, Kim! This is _____ giving you a call. You will remember that we met on October 15 at my presentation on lease options at your office. If you have sellers who are considering renting their homes if they do not sell soon, I would certainly love to work with you on finding a solution for their problem. Remember, when you work with me, you get your commission fast and in full. So, if you have some lease option prospects in mind, please give me a call at _____. Thanks.

If business has been done with a realtor, they will still need reminders — and probably appreciate them since they are getting help earning commissions. When calling say,

> Hi, George! This is _____. Hey, I just wanted to thank you for your business and let you know that I am looking for another lease purchase opportunity. If you have any sellers right now who would benefit from an option, please let me know. Give me a call at ___ _____. Hope you have had a great week! Look forward to hearing from you!

Of course, the key in working with real estate agents lies in one's actions. Be ethical and honest in all dealings. In the first place, it is the right thing to do. Second, the realtors' reputations are on the line. Their success depends upon a good reputation. And, remember, realtors have a grapevine that spreads news faster than the speed of light. Once word gets out that a person is unethical, that individual is effectively done in the market. Also, remember that realtors control upwards of 90 percent of the market. The dumbest thing to do is treat them badly. It is important to keep one's word on every deal and keep them informed of what happens on every lead. Follow up and tell them what has been done with a lead; for example, tell them that the property has been looked at and whether or not there is any interest. If not interested, be sure to explain why; for example, tell them in nice terms that it doesn't fit the needs, but that the lead is certainly appreciated and others are welcomed. In some cases, the agent may know that the property is overpriced but will still want an offer from an investor. He or she can then show it to the seller to convince them to reduce their price to a realistic level and a sale. The investor does not end up with the lease option, but he or she helped the agent make a sale and the realtor will remember that. Think of it as an added value service that is an investment in a long-term relationship with the realtor.

LANDLORDS

There are different types of landlords and each are motivated to sell for a variety of reasons. One type is the amateur who has watched too many infomercials about an easy way to make millions. These individuals soon find headaches they never imagined — bad tenants, ignorance of state and federal laws, tax complications, etc. After a while, all they want is out. The second type is professional landlords who are retiring or are simply burned out. They may not need the money from the sale of their property or may not even want to receive it yet because they'll incur a big capital gains bill if they do so. In cases like this, they would prefer to option the property to an investor and take advantage of the 1031 Tax-Deferred Exchange law. This tax law allows a person to sell one property and buy another without incurring capital gains taxes. All the profits simply have to be re-invested into the next property or properties within a specific timeline. The new properties have to be of equal or greater value. In this instance, the tax is deferred into the future, not eliminated. It is a win-win situation. Those who decide to move beyond lease options into a buy and hold strategy will definitely want to take advantage of it.

Of course, landlords may need some convincing about the arrangement, especially if they are ignorant about lease options and their benefits. That is where a bit of good, old-fashioned selling technique comes in handy. As we stated earlier, the benefits should be stressed to the customer and the question *What's in it for me?* should be answered. Benefits answer that question. Typical benefits are: saving money, making money, more convenience, more security, less hassle, etc. Specific benefits for landlords in terms of lease options include the following:

- **No maintenance hassles.** Tell the landlord, "As part of the deal, I will assume the maintenance work. That means you won't be getting any more aggravating phone calls at all times of the night or day."

- **No showings.** Tell the landlord, "I will handle all showings so you don't have the inconvenience of taking time out your evenings and weekends to do them. You will be freed of considerable aggravation and have less stress in your life."

- **No advertising costs/hassles.** Tell the landlord, "I assume all advertising costs and will handle all calls regarding the property. Your time is your own again and you have eliminated a business expense."

- **Timely rent.** Tell the landlord, "With me, you get a monthly check every time, on time, regardless of whether or not the tenant has paid me on time. You have the security of knowing that this income is guaranteed every month."

- **Vacancies.** Tell the landlord, "I pay whether the home is vacant or not. Your rent is guaranteed."

Benefits like these can be a powerful inducement to a tired or retiring landlord. They will be willing to lease the property for less money. By negotiating a lower payment with the seller, the property can then be rented and a good cash flow can be obtained.

QUALIFIED SELLERS

Unqualified sellers can waste one's time and money and delay the identification of qualified and interested parties. It is in the investor's interest right from the start to qualify sellers. This can be done by first looking for two categories of sellers. The first is individuals who do not need the cash out of the home to move on. The second is individuals who do not have any equity in their property. They have 100 percent financing. We will deal with the second category in this section. Generally speaking, these types will be found:

- **Inheritance sellers** — These are individuals who have inherited a property and who do not want the complications of maintaining and/or marketing that property. Through a lease option, they can be relieved of these complications. One caution: Limit these transactions to situations where there is only one or two inheritors. The more inheritors, the thornier the deal can become because of the usual family entanglements.

- **"Veteran" homeowners** — By "veteran," we mean owners who have owned their property for a long time. Often, they are financially stable, have low monthly payments, and have a good savings cushion. This means they can buy a new home without selling the old one. This situation enables the investor to get a lower payment as well. The result is good cash flow.

- **New home builders** — These individuals have built a new home, but their old property has not sold yet. They do not want to pay for a vacant property. If the old home does not move quickly, they become more anxious to get it off their hands. They are motivated sellers — ideal candidates for a lease option.

- **Recently married individuals** — In cases like this, the seller may have moved into their spouse's home and they certainly do not enjoy paying for property that is vacant. A lease option is a win-win for everyone involved. The seller is relieved of the burden of paying for the original property and the investor is dealing with an individual who had the financial capacity to pay for that property. Responsible people are being dealt with.

- **Transferred individuals** — We have mentioned this

type earlier, but it bears repeating here. Transferees — especially those who are now out-of- state — may be anxious for a lease option because they do not want the burden of double payments. They may also like a lease option because they simply do not know how long the job will last or if it will work out at all. There is a lot of anxiety and an investor can help reduce or eliminate that anxiety by offering them a lease option.

There is a common characteristic among all these types — low debt. This means the investor avoids dealing with individuals who have financial difficulties and can be risky choices for lease options.

Human beings are being dealt with, many of whom have pride of ownership, so they cannot be expected to accept a lease option on the spot. Many will require persuasion and that is where salesmanship comes in. We stated earlier that an investor should emphasize benefits in any conversation with a prospective seller or buyer. This concept is so important that we will emphasize it here once again. Keep the following slogan in mind every time a customer is contacted:

PEOPLE BUY BENEFITS!

CHAPTER 10

SELLING YOURSELF & YOUR DEALS

Entrepreneurship means good salesmanship. All deals begin with people, not buildings or income projections. To make money, you first have to sell your ideas to interested parties. It pays to present those ideas in a compelling way. Selling is definitely a skill that can be learned with practice. This chapter will provide you with guidelines on the basics of salesmanship. If you are a person who prefers a structured learning environment, there are many courses and seminars available on the market that will provide you with proven skill models and techniques. After you learn those skills, you can adapt them to your personal style and make them a natural part of your interactions with prospects and clients.

GUIDELINE 1: ALWAYS STRESS BENEFITS

In any presentation or deal, you need to answer the prospect's unspoken question, "What is in it for me?" Depending on the person, benefits may vary. One person may want to make money and another may want to save money by cutting costs. Determine which benefits matter the most to the person. A significant part of determining needs comes from listening and asking good questions.

GUIDELINE 2: DO NOT BE A GOOD LISTENER —
BE A GREAT ONE

Listen closely to the prospect's needs. Nothing is worse than making a presentation to a prospect and getting this response, "You have not really heard what I have been saying, have you?" In other words, you have done all the talking and missed the mark. Below are the basic guidelines for effective listening. Remember, clients are paying you to listen to them talk about their needs and problems. Therefore, it is common sense to listen well. It results in income and repeat business. Therefore, follow these basic principles:

Listen twice as much as you talk. Particularly in initial meetings with prospects, listen closely and keep your talk to a minimum for two benefits. First, it establishes you as being concerned more about the prospect's needs than your own. Second, it allows you to discover exactly what the prospect's needs are so you can tailor your benefits to meet those needs.

Make use of prompts. A prompt is a simple technique to keep prospects talking. A prompt is a short interjection, such as: "Go on. Uh-huh. Tell me more."

Use positive body language. Show a relaxed yet alert posture to demonstrate that you are interested in what the prospect has to say and that you are paying close attention. Part of positive body language is making good eye contact. Other indicators of interest are nodding your head, subtly leaning toward them, and writing down what they say.

Use short summaries. At strategic times during a conversation, briefly summarize what the prospect has said up to that point. It could be something like, "Kim, I see that you are careful to keep costs down." A short summary is a great tool for two reasons. One, it tells the prospect that you are listening closely. Second, if you have gotten off track, it gives them an opportunity to correct any misconceptions you may have and that gets you back on track.

Do not go overboard on these techniques. For example, if you keep interrupting a prospect to make summaries, you will simply be an irritation. Instead, work to use them at strategic points. With practice, you will find that you can slip them into your conversations in a natural way that will fit your style.

GUIDELINE 3: ASK GOOD QUESTIONS

Good questions have two purposes. One, they get you the information you need to meet the need of your prospects. Two, they demonstrate your knowledge of commercial real estate investments. By asking sharp, perceptive questions, you show prospects and clients that they can trust your expertise. Reams and reams of paper have been devoted to the subject of questioning; however, the technique boils down to two types of questions, and each type has a specific purpose.

Open questions elicit general information and encourage a prospect to open up about his or her needs. They are ideal to use at the beginning of your first visit with a client. Open questions often begin with words like, "How," "What," "Why," or, "In what way." Examples are:

- "What are your goals for this project?
- "Why are the rent rolls a concern for you?"
- "In what ways do you want to use this property?" **105**

Closed questions ask for *specific information* and are designed to get at the root of an opportunity, problem, or need. It is best to use them after you have established rapport with a prospect and want to pin down specific needs so you can come up with a custom-tailored approach to the situation. Closed questions can often be answered with a yes or a no. They might sound like this:

- "Do you need more parking space for this restaurant?"

- "Are you having problems with this tenant?"

- "Did you have a good experience with this architect?"

Of course, no conversation ever proceeds in a straight line so keep in mind that you will always be using a mixture of open and closed questions. With practice, you will be able to make questioning an easy and natural part of your interactions with prospects and clients.

GUIDELINE 4: ALWAYS BE PREPARED

When you approach potential investors, they expect you to be fully prepared. Why should they expect otherwise? After all, it is their money on the line. Therefore, approach every presentation and other meetings by making sure you are fully versed in every aspect of your proposal. If it is a large, complicated proposal, plan it carefully and go through dry runs to make sure you are confident in your presentation skills. If you are new to the field or not fully confident, ask colleagues and friends to review your presentation. Have them throw random questions at you so you get used to the process. This process is important for two reasons. One, investors and others will often throw questions at you to test your knowledge of the field and the project, particularly if they do not know you well. Second, few meetings proceed in a straight line; through practice, you will be able to handle random questions with ease.

GUIDELINE 5: BRING ENERGY

One of the hallmarks of leaders is that, when they walk into a room, they bring energy with them. As a commercial real estate investor, you are a leader. You have the ability to inspire a vision in others, your own employees, prospects, and clients. If you are honestly enthusiastic about a project and communicate that enthusiasm clearly, your attitude of quiet confidence and enthusiasm in every aspect of your presentation will be contagious.

GUIDELINE 6: BE VISUAL

It is no secret that a picture is worth a thousand words. So, it is always good to be visual in whatever materials you present to prospects and clients. In your presentations, you want to paint a picture for your audience that clearly and quickly allows them to grasp the central idea of your project. Since visuals can be so compelling, they need to reflect a professional image and to be prepared by professional graphic artists who know how to make the best impact on an audience. Visuals are no longer as expensive as they used to be. Thanks to the Internet, you can submit bids worldwide and get the best combination of price and quality. Two sources of freelance commercial artists, graphic designers, and writers are elance.com (**www.elance.com**) and sologig. com. (**www.sologig.com**). Of course, you can also go local to find these services if you prefer closer contact with service providers.

GUIDELINE 7: CONCENTRATE ON MAIN POINTS

Do not overwhelm your prospect or client with a ton of technical information (unless they are technically inclined). People can absorb only so much information during a meeting. Instead, concentrate on presenting the main, attractive points of your proposal. You want potential investors to leave any meeting with those main points stuck clearly in their minds. Speak clearly and directly. Avoid using technical terms or trying to sound like a college professor. Your audience is not interested in flowery, vague language; they want information that will help them make the right decision.

GUIDELINE 8: USE THE PROSPECT'S OR CLIENT'S LANGUAGE AS MUCH AS POSSIBLE

Every industry has its jargon and "insider" terms. The purpose of learning this specialist language is so that you can increase the comfort level with everyone you meet. For example, if an investor prefers "contracts" instead of "deals," then use contract, or when speaking with an architect or engineer, know some of their language. As you gain experience, you will learn all the basic technical terms and be able to create a comfort level with everyone you meet.

GUIDELINE 9: BE HONEST AND FORTHRIGHT

With any business deal, it is all about building relationships on trust. Be honest and forthright in all your dealings. Honesty will convince investors and others to do business with you now and in the future. No one wants to invest capital in a dishonest person's project; it is throwing money down the drain. In commercial real estate investment, where a lot of money can be at stake, a golden reputation is one of your best assets.

GUIDELINE 10: ALWAYS DEAL WITH THE DECISION-MAKER

Investors sometimes try to sell a non decision-maker on a project, wasting time. They have not done their homework on the prospect or client. While they are dealing with an underling, another investor may be talking with the decision-maker. You will save yourself frustration by identifying the decision-maker early in the process and then making your presentation to that person. If you have levels of bureaucracy to wade through, be politely patient and persistent. The decision-maker may want to determine if you are truly committed to your project and have the skill and determination to fight your way to the top.

GUIDELINE 11: ALWAYS DRESS AND ACT APPROPRIATELY FOR THE SITUATION

Match your clothing and personal style to your audience. If you are dealing with a farmer or rancher, it is appropriate to wear open-necked shirts, jeans, and work boots. If you are dealing with big investors for, say, a shopping mall development, you would choose a well-tailored suit and tie. It is all part of making a great first impression. If investors and others do not feel that you are part of their group, you will have a tough time selling your ideas to them.

Here is an example: An investor, tired from a long business trip, approached the owner of a large poultry operation about a land deal. The owner was a big man dressed in overalls and workbooks. From the beginning, he was hostile to the investor. The investor could not figure out why he was making such a bad impression until he looked down and realized he had forgotten to change clothes. He was wearing a three-piece business suit, a tie, and shiny shoes. The owner had been suspicious immediately because the investor's clothing indicated he did not know a thing about agricultural operations. The deal never got off the ground.

Subtly adapt your style to match that of your audience. For example, a rural prospect or client may want to take his time to discuss the weather or local happenings before getting down to business. At the other end of the spectrum, a busy urban prospect will most likely want to get to business immediately. Usually, you can get a sense of a person's style quickly through the setting in which you find yourself.

GUIDELINE 12: DO NOT CUT DOWN YOUR COMPETITION; TALK IT UP.

In an earlier guideline, we mentioned the importance of trust. One way to destroy that trust is to speak negatively of the competition. If you do that, prospects and clients will assume that you will do the same of them and will not want to do business with you. Always say good things about your competition.

GUIDELINE 13: ASK FOR COMMITMENT

If you have done your homework and made a great presentation, you have a right to close on a deal. Never be afraid to ask for commitment. If you do not ask, you will not receive. Here is one proven sales technique for closing: Toward the end of your presentation, briefly summarize the main needs of the prospect or client and the benefits that meet those needs, and then ask for commitment to the deal. This technique accomplishes two important goals. First, of course, you may get the deal on the spot. Second, if the prospect or client hesitates or does not want to sign immediately, any doubts or objections will surface, and you can deal with them on the spot.

For example, you can say, "George, I can see that you some doubts. Tell me about them now so I can answer any questions you have." Or you might be direct and ask, "Mary, what are your objections to this project?" She may say the cost is too high or the design is objectionable — far preferable to leaving the meeting and not knowing exactly why the presentation failed. Any good salesperson will tell you it is better to find out about doubts and objections right away so you can handle them. You may not convince the person in that particular meeting, but doing so provides you with ammunition for the next meeting.

GUIDELINE 14: ALWAYS FOLLOW UP

No matter who you are dealing with, always follow up with them. You want to keep your name constantly in their minds. Follow up can take many forms. It can be as simple as a phone call to say hello and see how things are going in their business or personal lives, or it can be as sophisticated as checking on the details of a project. If appropriate, add a personal touch. It never hurts to send birthday or anniversary cards or congratulations on a successful deal. Another good follow-up technique is to provide prospects and clients with information of interest to them. For example, if you have a lead and you know it is not in your area of interest, send it to them. They will appreciate the thoughtfulness and will reciprocate down the line with a lead for you. On a more   **111** general level, you can send them articles or books concerning their specialty. With this technique, you are increasing their knowledge and demonstrating that you keep up with the latest developments in the field of commercial real estate investment. Remember this variation on an earlier statement: *Success is all about building great relationships in the business community.*

CHAPTER 11

CONVENTIONAL FINANCING FOR COMMERCIAL REAL ESTATE INVESTMENTS

You want to use other people's money (OPM) to gain leverage in your financing. OPM money can come from a variety of conventional sources (mortgages from banks, credit unions, and other major financial institutions) or equity sources (REITs, partnerships, and corporations). Depending on the type and stage of a project, loans will either be short-term or long-term. On any given project, you will be using a combination of these loans. In this chapter, we will look at loans available from conventional sources. (Equity financing will be the subject of the next chapter.)

SHORT-TERM LOANS

In development projects, short-term loans fall into four categories. An *interim* loan is designed to fill the gap from construction start to the point at which tenant occupancy occurs. This type of loan may range from one to three years or more, depending on the size and complexity of the project. Here is an example: Assume you want to build an office complex. To fund it you need a permanent mortgage that will fund $1 million when the complex is 80 percent occupied. From start of construction until that 80 percent occupancy is achieved, assume the mortgage is only $700,000; therefore, you arrange an interim loan of $300,000 to cover that period of time.

There is also a *gap* loan, which covers the gap between equity and permanent financing. Often, it is a seller carry-back loan (financed by the seller) or a land loan. A variation of the short-term construction loan is the *roll-over* loan. In this case, the bank allows the initial loan (interest only) to be rolled over into an amortizing loan, usually for a three- to five-year period. The advantage is that it gives a developer a good buffer against securing permanent financing that can be much more expensive. For example, if the current market has high rates, the developer can use the time provided by a roll-over loan to shop for lower rates on permanent loans.

The fourth loan in this category is the *permanent* or *"take-out"* loan. It is designed to pay off the interim or construction loan. Terms can range from three to thirty years, so that a take-out loan can be a long-term loan.

Commercial banks offer most of these loans restricted to 75 percent of verifiable costs with the stipulation that you substantiate that you are able to pay the balance of the cost of the project in cash. Typically, the terms of these loans range from 12 to 36 months with interest rates in the range of 1 to 1.5 percent higher than the permanent loan market. Banks charge one point (1 percent) up front as a commitment fee. They also stipulate that the borrower(s) provide a personal guarantee. Finally, they will require a minimum pre-leasing occupancy to break even. A typical approach in this area

is a 75 percent of value or cost interim loan coupled with a permanent loan of 75 percent to 80 percent of the projected value at completion.

LONG-TERM LOANS

These are permanent loans offered by "institutional" sources — banks, savings and loans, REITs, trusts, or insurance companies. Terms on these loans can be up to 30 years. They can be new loans, refinanced loans, or take-out loans. Normally, a permanent loan has two parts. One is the "note," or the loan document itself. The other part is the security document — mortgage or deed of trust, depending on the area where you live. The security document lists the lender's rights in the event of a default. The mortgage usually is recorded as a lien against the deed of the property *when it is funded* in the eastern part of the United States. In the western part, the deed of trust is recorded against the title at *the close of escrow*.

The *note* outlines business points and includes such information as names and addresses of the parties involved, the name and address of the real property, the amount and terms of the loan, the interest rate and amortization schedule, the amount and number of payments, due dates, late dates, penalties, and the signatures of the parties.

The *deed of trust* or *mortgage* elaborates on the note. In other words, it adds conditions to the loan. Common conditions include tenancy changes, insurance, prohibitions against assignment and transferability, and requirements that the borrower assign all leases to the lender.

OTHER TYPES OF FINANCING

In addition to the loans described above, there are many

other types of financing available for your projects. Below we provide a description of the more common forms of alternative financing.

Equity Financing

Equity financing is money raised specially for a project through means of joint ventures, partnerships, corporations, and limited liability companies. It is not backed by a lien on the property; instead, equity financing is aimed at participation in the profits once the project is completed. Equity financing offers a broad range of options. We will cover this subject in more detail in the next chapter in terms of partnerships, syndication, and public financing.

- **Land subordinations** — In this case, the seller (lender) stipulates that his note becomes a subordinate lien to new construction financing. For all practical purposes, this is a joint venture because the seller's equity is used to fill the gap in cash investment required by the construction lender. In essence, the developer pays interest due on the note and profit participation as soon the property is sold. For example, after a housing developer sells his lots, the lender shares in the profits. The benefit for the developer is that it affords leverage. It can be a win-win deal for both parties when the deal is a good one. On the downside, if a deal goes bad, the seller may have to handle defaults on the construction loan to preserve equity in the land loan. If the seller does not do so, the institution can face foreclosure from the construction lender.

- **Land leases** — These are available for commercial

properties. They can be subordinated or unsubordinated. A *subordinated land lease* operates in much the same fashion as a subordinated land loan. The main difference is that it is used mainly for long-term ownership projects. It is a profit-sharing agreement. The lessor participates in the venture's profits above the lease payment — a good deal, as rent normally increases over the years and the property appreciates as well. *Unsubordinated land leases* are available as well, but they are few and far between because lenders do not want to make land lease payments if a loan default occurs or face a loss through foreclosure.

- **Participating loans** — From the lenders' point of view, the purpose of a participation loan is to get increased yield on their loan dollars. Such loans are often made when the developer does not meet the credit standards of the lender. To offset increased risk, the lender makes an agreement whereby the yield is boosted in the later years of the mortgage.

Loan Renewals

Short-term ten-year loans are available for commercial real estate investment. Lenders like them because they can charge higher fees, and there are fewer troubles with such loans. Lenders know that most properties will have great appreciation over a decade. Rents will rise as well, usually by an average of 35 to 40 percent or more. This result is increased cash flow. Increased operating expenses are offset because many of these expenses are passed on to tenants. If lenders see all these factors coming together, they may be willing to refinance at a lower rate to the developer, freeing cash for the developer who can keep the original property while buying or building other properties, and there are no tax consequences.

Exit Strategies

The exit strategy you choose depends on the goals for your career and how far you are along in that career. You can sell and take the profits, but you will be paying taxes on your gain. You can sell and exchange for another property, or you can keep your current property and refinance it. That way you can broaden your holdings without suffering any tax liabilities. Another advantage of this last strategy is that you can diversify your portfolio, which means greater safety for your investments. The disadvantage is that your portfolio becomes more complex and takes more of your time and energy. You should have an exit strategy in mind from the moment you build or buy any property and it should relate to the goals you set for yourself in your investment career.

CHAPTER 12

EQUITY FINANCING OF COMMERCIAL REAL ESTATE INVESTMENTS

You will normally need a combination of conventional and equity financing for your investments and projects. Equity financing simply means that you find people who want to invest money in your projects and reap a profit from that investment. You have a number of sources from which to obtain money since investors love real estate for two reasons: One, it is real; that is, land is around forever in human terms, and buildings are physical assets that last a long time; two, real estate is "lienable;" that is, if things go bad, investors have a claim against the property and can regain some or all their investment. This means investors have greater security and less risk as opposed to investing in common stock.

One source for obtaining money is partnerships, both general and limited. We will discuss this business entity in more detail in the next chapter, but it is the simplest and often the best route to take. You will have your own money and the money of others invested in your projects.

PRIVATE FUNDING SOURCES

When you obtain funds from private sources, it is often called "private placement." Most often, ground rules are laid out for the participation of investors. For example, investors must meet a minimum net worth requirement, and they must be knowledgeable about commercial real estate ventures. Obviously, you do not want amateurs involved in your business transactions.

To gain funds from private investors you can stress benefits that include instant return on investment (ROI), appreciation, tax write-offs, and capital gains, or exchange at the end of the deal. When you present these benefits to investors, along with a sound, compelling business plan, you will have an interested audience.

Parameters of partnerships vary, but there are common elements. *One*, they stipulate a specific dollar amount to be paid into a deal to form the partnership. *Two*, there is an annual preferred return based on a fixed percentage on paid-in equity. When the equity is partially repaid, the investor's return is based on the remaining investment. When the equity is repaid completely, there is no preferred return. *Three*, the annual return is sometimes cumulative but not always. *Four*, the annual rate of return is paid against one-half of the annual cash flow. *Five*, on sale or refinancing, the investor's capital is repaid before any profit distribution. Of course, along with these considerations, you must take into account any fees paid for management, brokerage, or development services.

Private placement is often the preferred way to obtain funds for your projects. However, if you are not able to obtain private funding for some reason, you can tap into public funding sources.

PUBLIC FUNDING SOURCES

Public funding is obtained through the sale of stocks and bonds, with the sale of common stock being the most universal method of obtaining capital in the United States. Publicly-held real estate corporations tend to concentrate on the residential market, however. They are more interested in cash flow than in investment property. As you will see in the next chapter, the corporate form of ownership can have significant costs and considerable public scrutiny.

Another form of public ownership is the REIT, the real estate investment trust, companies that own real estate and related assets. Many REITs make their money by buying real estate properties and then renting them out to corporations and consumers. An REIT allows the average investor the opportunity to participate in the commercial real estate market without getting deeply involved in the process. They trust others to manage their investments for them. REITs tend to specialize in housing, mortgage bonds, office properties, and retail complexes.

For the investor, an REIT offers several advantages. One is the yield on the investment. A company must return at least 90 percent of its earnings to its shareholders in the form of dividends to qualify as an REIT for tax purposes. As of this writing, the average REIT provides around 6 percent plus annual dividend yield. A second advantage is that REITs are not as sensitive to market ups and downs as other investments are, so they can provide the investor with portfolio diversification and more predictable returns.

A third advantage is that REITs own "hard" assets, such as land and buildings. Moreover, they often sign their tenants to long-term lease contracts. The advantage of this is that REITs tend to be stable, providing security to the investor.

REITs do have disadvantages for investors. Only 10 percent of their annual profits can be reinvested to back into their core business lines on a yearly basis. Therefore, they tend to grow more slowly than average stocks, and dividend payments are not guaranteed to investors. The real estate market has its downturns, and REITs can be affected by these economic slowdowns. A final disadvantage relates to the REITs' tax-advantaged status. They are allowed to deduct the dividends they pay out from their taxable income. Therefore, from an investor's point of view, this means that about two-thirds of all dividends paid by REITs do not qualify for the lower 15 percent tax rate implemented by Congress. Most non-REITs qualify for this low rate.

We advise that you stick to the partnership business form, especially if you are new to the field. It will help you learn commercial real estate investment, and the experience you gain will be valuable as you progress in your career.

If you would like additional information on REITs, I suggest *The Complete Guide to Investing in Reits − Real Estate Investment Trust: How to Earn High Rates of Return Safely*, available from Atlantic Publishing Company (**www.atlantic-pub.com**).

CHAPTER 13

TYPES OF OWNERSHIP IN COMMERCIAL REAL ESTATE INVESTMENTS

There are many business structures available to you as an investor in commercial real estate. The type you choose depends on your circumstances. This chapter outlines the most common forms of ownership and their advantages and disadvantages so you can select the one that best meets your goals and financial capacity.

PARTNERSHIPS

Partnerships consist of two or more partners who want to work together on real estate investments. Often partners pool their capital and take on whatever responsibilities best suit their talents. For example, one might be the marketer, while the other handles financing. Partners may not actually have the title or ownership directly in acquired properties. Instead, they own a partnership interest. For example, they may pro-rate the ownership according to the cash contributions each of them has made. Partnerships usually take one of two forms.

General Partnerships

In this setup, either partner can act on behalf of the partnership: Each possesses the right to participate fully in property management and operations. There are several advantages to a general partnership: *First*, they are easy to establish and maintain. There is no need to register with your state and pay fees, as you have to do in the establishment of a corporation or limited liability company (LLC). *Second*, income tax returns can be filed with ease, relatively speaking, because general partnerships are normally "pass through" tax entities. What this means is that the partners, not the partnership, are taxed. *Third*, unlike a regular corporation, there is no need to file separate tax returns for the corporate entity and its owners. *Fourth*, general partnerships offer great flexibility in terms of assigning responsibilities and benefits. You can respond more readily when the needs of the business change. As stated earlier, this flexibility extends to distribution of profits and losses. For example, if you are a partner and take on more financial risk, you can receive higher profits than your partner. *Fifth*, a partnership is legally considered a discrete asset so that you can transfer assets to other people, heirs, or estates. The partnership agreement usually limits the terms of transference.

General partnerships also have their *disadvantages*. You want to enter into a general partnership only with people you trust. That is because one business-related act of a partner can make you and all other partners legally liable. You can prevent or limit the damage from this kind of problem with a carefully written partnership agreement. It should establish each partner's day-to-day duties, share of profits or losses, and what happens if one partner dies or retires.

Limited Partnerships

The roles and responsibilities of the partners distinguish this type of partnership from a general partnership. Often, a limited partnership consists of one or more general partners and one or more limited partners. Typically, the general partners run the operations of the business while the limited partners provide capital and help arrange financing but do not take an active role in running the business so that the limited partners are "passive" investors and receive a share of the profits because they provided capital. Statutes regarding limited partnerships vary by state, and you must check with the appropriate government agency for a definition of the obligations and responsibilities of the partners. The partnership is required to file with the secretary of state and must also file various reports.

A key feature of a limited partnership agreement concerns the area of liability. Typically, it falls on the general partners and not on limited partners. For this reason, investors are reluctant to be general partners. However, general partners can form a corporation or limited liability companies (LLC) to reduce liability. Although limited partners may not participate in day-to-day running of the business, they generally have the right to participate in and vote on major decisions that affect the partnership.

There are many *advantages* to a limited partnership. *First,* if you are a limited partner, you can invest even though you do not have expertise or the time to devote to the day-to-day operation of the business. *Second,* if you are a limited partner, you take on the financial risk but not the liability risk. *Third,* partners are able to allocate profits, losses, and gains as they see fit, regardless of the equity interest of a specific partner (subject to compliance with tax laws). *Fourth,* general partners prepare an IRS Form 1065 for the partnership, permitting each partner to prepare his or her own tax form listing all profits, losses, and depreciations. *Fifth,* a limited partnership is a "pass through" operation, meaning that all profits pass through to the partners who then include their allocated income on their personal tax returns. *Sixth*, it is much easier to attract investors as limited partners. *Seventh*, it permits general partners to use their expertise, make key decisions, and manage the business. *Eighth*, limited partners can leave the business as they see fit, or they can be replaced without the need for dissolution the limited partnership.

LIMITED LIABILITY COMPANIES

This is a popular hybrid business ownership structure. It combines the properties of a corporation and partnership. It is popular for several reasons. *First*, it provides the flexibility and tax advantages of a partnership while maintaining the limited liability benefits of a corporation. Similar to a corporation, an LLC is a separate legal entity that provides limited liability to its members. At the same time, it has the tax benefits of a partnership. *Second*, LLCs are free of the paperwork and legal requirements of corporations (annual reports, director meetings, and shareholder requirements). *Third*, LLCs are a "pass through" tax entity, which means company profits and losses are passed through the business and taxed solely on the members' individual tax returns. *Fourth*, members of an LLC can hire a management group to run the business, consisting of members, nonmembers, or a combination of both. *Fifth*, members can split profits and losses any way they wish. *Sixth*, dividend distribution is nontaxable. *Seventh*, an unlimited number of members may join a single LLC, and most states allow single-member LLCs. *Eighth*, an LLC may affiliate with other businesses, unlike an S corporation, where that ability is limited.

126 There are disadvantages to an LLC. For one thing, costs can

be higher. That is because some states impose income or franchise taxes on LLCs or require LLCs to pay annual fees to operate in that state. For another, there is a lack of legal precedent. LLCs have existed as legal business entities only since 1996. That means there is not much legal precedent available to help you predict how disputes may affect your business. Therefore, if you are considering forming or joining an LLC, check first with an attorney who specializes in this area to advise you.

CORPORATIONS

A corporation is a legal entity owned by one or more shareholders who provide money in the form of common or preferred stock to establish and sustain a corporation. In effect, they are owners of the corporation. They profit when the price of the stock rises or suffer a loss when the price falls. Corporations can be public or private (closed). As an investor, you create your own private or closely held corporation by filing articles of incorporation and bylaws with the appropriate state agency. Requirements for incorporation vary by state. That means you should study these requirements carefully before forming a corporation.

An advantage of a corporation is that it provides you with a pool of capital to form the business. It can be easier to gather money from a large number of investors than from other sources. From the shareholders' point of view, it offers limited liability. Since the owners of a corporation actually own stock and not real estate, the most shareholders can lose is their equity investment. There are also disadvantages. From your point of view as an investor, it can be expensive in terms of initial set-up. You will need to pay an attorney to draw up the organizational documents. There are also regulatory costs. To maintain corporate status, you will need to adhere to the extensive reporting requirements at state and federal levels. If these requirements are not met or if there is lack of capital, creditors or lien holders can seek personal liability for individual shareholders.

There are two types of corporations available to you.

C Corporations: They have the advantage of continuity (they continue in the event a shareholder dies). However, there is a major disadvantage. They are taxed twice, once when the business makes a profit and then a second time when those profits are distributed to shareholders. Another disadvantage is that if the corporation has losses, it has to carry them over to the next tax year because the shareholders cannot use C corporation losses on their personal returns.

S Corporations: A major advantage of the S corporation is that it avoids double taxation by passing all tax liabilities onto shareholders. As such, S corporations are only taxed once. However, they are seldom used in real estate ownership for a good reason — the liquidation of an S corporation is a taxable event, meaning that even if the shareholders agree to an equitable distribution of assets, the Internal Revenue Service will consider the liquidation as taxable. The shareholders will then be forced to pay capital gains taxes and possibly sell some of the assets. In addition, there is the issue of material participation, an IRS term that indicates whether an investor worked and was involved in a business activity on a regular basis. It has a series of tests to determine material participation which affects the tax benefits you may or may not receive.

Incorporation is an expensive choice for holding real estate assets for a commercial real estate investor. The primary negative is double taxation of profits depending on the form of incorporation. You must be willing to pay for the professional, legal, and accounting advice not only at the beginning but also on a continual basis. These expenses can mount up. You also have to deal with the hassle of ongoing technical requirements and the possible expensive possibility of double taxation. We recommend you choose one of the other forms of ownership described in this chapter.

CHAPTER 14

COMMERCIAL REAL ESTATE LOAN DOCUMENTS

As you might expect, it is vital to understand every aspect of the documents and agreements generated in the process of obtaining funding for your projects. You do not want to be a lamb among wolves when it comes to putting your name on a loan form. This chapter will describe the process and common documents and agreements involved in commercial real estate transactions.

THE PROCESS

First, it is important to know the difference between two important positions in the lending market, *mortgage bankers* and *mortgage brokers*. Mortgage bankers represent most commercial lenders. They operate on behalf of a fixed number of lenders and often have a long-standing relationship with them. Mortgage brokers are "shoppers." That is, they shop your loan application around and operate on a deal-by-deal basis. We recommend that you use a mortgage banker who knows whether there are lenders interested in your type of project. In short, they can steer you to the right person. Mortgage bankers are also likely to be more well-connected within the financial community. By contrast, mortgage brokers may send your application out willy-nilly, wasting time. Brokers also tend to be more expensive for this reason: The broker charges you a fee for finding a mortgage banker; the banker then charges you a fee. You end up paying twice. If you decide to work with a mortgage broker, be clear on what the fees are up front and insist that the broker stick to that amount.

The first step in obtaining funds is the loan application. The mortgage banker or broker prepares it for you, and you execute it. The term for this is "origination." Be clear on the type of loan you require. For example, as discussed earlier, if you are planning a development project, you will need two types of loans — the construction (interim) interest-only loan and the permanent (take-out) fully-amortized loan. The construction loan will require full payment within one to three years. The permanent loan will range from 10 to 30 years. If, on the other hand, you are interested in an existing project, you will apply directly for a permanent loan.

In terms of construction loans, it is most likely you will apply directly to the lender, often banks that specialize in this area. To find one, check the Yellow Pages or talk to a mortgage banker who may arrange for a construction loan if you are going through him or her for the take-out loan. Expect mortgage bankers to stipulate a good percentage of pre-leasing and actual cash as part of the loan arrangement. They will want to see that you are experienced in the field or have deep pockets. They will also want to see that you have strong, experienced contractors lined up for the project. Any loan you obtain will have a specified interest rate, or it will float over the bank's prime rate. The bank will collect its interest on a monthly basis from the proceeds of the loan draw. In addition, they will have a third party, such as an inspection service, certify your loan draw requests. To sum up, a lender will impose specific conditions, and you must meet them before he or she will agree to fund your project. From your point of view, you want any contract drawn up to be clear and understandable. Avoid any contract that is vague or so general that it allows the lender to walk away from the deal before it is signed. This can happen if economic conditions take a sudden downturn.

The loan application should have specific terms laid out. It will include the project plans and specifications, financial projections, current and projected leasing terms and occupancy, and your financial statement.

More specifically, it will include the following:

- A file number and project reference
- An application deadline date
- Your name and legal identity
- Security specifics (mortgage, deed of trust)
- A data sheet (the financial condition of the principals, property management information, existing property debt, authorization for credit inquiries)
- Loan guarantee specifics
- Terms and conditions of the proposed loan (interest rate, payment terms, impound accounts for taxes and insurance)
- The application fee
- The commitment fee

- Specified conditions that must be met before closing (environmental reports and certification of architects and engineers)

- The broker's role and fees

- Cost breakdowns and who is responsible for specific payments

- Closing conditions (appraisal, required leases, lender's inspection, and architect and engineering report requirements)

- Lender's receipt

- Borrower's representation

- Any additional requirements

- Date

- Borrower's signature

- Legal description of property

Of course, as the borrower, you will be required to sign the document, but if you have formed a partnership or an LLC, the lender will want the signatures of everyone involved. This is a form of security for them. If there is misrepresentation, they can take action against all applicants.

In addition to the loan application, there will be a loan commitment. This is a rider attached to the application. It is often in the form of a letter and is addressed to the proposed buyer. A loan commitment letter includes such elements as the acceptance language, expiration date, required fees, payment dates, the specific closing date, signatures of lender and borrower, and additional conditions (for example, lender's approval of all leases).

Once you have gained commitment for a loan, you have to close on it. Loan closings are essential to your deals, of course, but be prepared for them to be a long and tedious process since there are so many people involved (the lender, the mortgage banker or broker, tenants, and so on). Our recommendation is to stay on top of closing participants right from the start. For example, estoppel certificates can be a problem. Tenants often want to renegotiate their leases when asked to execute these documents. Or they are simply slow in signing them. That means you have to "pester" them in order to get the certificates signed within a reasonable time.

THE PROMISSORY NOTE

A promissory note is a written promise to repay the loan. It is spelled out in specific terms. These terms will vary with the note, but they often include the following items:

- Date

- Borrower and lender names

- Address of lender

- The principal sum

- Interest rate

- Term

- Place of payment

- Terms of repayment

- Terms of late payment charges

- Promise to pay

- Acceleration and pre-payment stipulations

- Deed of trust or mortgage attached

- Attorney's fees and other boilerplate items

- Signatures and date

As stated above, terms will vary, so any promissory note you sign may have more than the basic elements just listed.

With any loan or promissory note, there is the matter of priority. Simply put, most loans stipulate that the lender has "first position." This is a protection for the lender and means that the lender's rights are subject only to the payment of real estate taxes. In other words, the lender has the ability to pay the taxes to protect his or her position. There are also "junior" positions — second, third, and so forth. If a lender is in second position, he or she has to bring the loan up to current status or pay it off to eliminate any default on that loan. Priority is determined by the date of recordation.

Of course, notes must be secured, which is done by the recording of the mortgage or deed of trust. In effect, they are liens against the property and are "security instruments." There are two purposes for the recording of these documents. One, it establishes the priority discussed above. Two, it makes public the fact that the lien exists. This allows prospective lenders to determine the priority of the lien in regard to any proposed financing. As stated earlier, whether a mortgage or deed of trust is involved depends on the area of the country in which you live. Eastern states tend to use the traditional mortgage format, while western states, on the other hand, use the deed of trust. Since both formats serve the same function (lien recordation), the differences lie mainly in the manner in which they are drawn up. In mortgage states, an attorney is required to prepare the document. In deed of trust states, it can be drawn up by a title company. Either way, expect the mortgage or deed of trust document to be detailed, long, and non-negotiable. Both these security instruments are universal to all real estate property borrowing and are often standardized. They include such information as:

- The account number

- Borrower's name and mailing address

- Beneficiary's name and mailing address

- Trustee's name and mailing address

- The date

- Property description (location, town, county, state, address, and so on)

- Note amount

- Purpose of the document ("recitals")

- Terms and conditions

- Mutual agreements (rights of assignment, damages, trespass, personal guarantees, and so on)

- Additional security (if required)

- Default provisions and remedies

- Recording authority

- Successors in interest

- Rights of assignment

- Signatures and date

Be aware that special provisions may be added to the general terms of the mortgage or deed of trust. For example, there is the matter of cross collateralization. In this instance, a borrower has more than one property and offers them as collateral for the loan. So, the mortgage or deed of trust is recorded against all these properties. Thus, when any of these collateralized properties are sold, the proceeds go to the lender before any payment is made to the borrower. Another example of a special provision is the personal guarantee. This may occur when the borrower does not have enough collateral to secure the note in full. He or she is required to pay the difference of the short fall. In general, personal guarantees are best avoided. The lender can require you to pay the note in full. The result may be that you end up broke and stuck with the property.

CHAPTER 15

THE ALL-IMPORTANT TOPIC OF LEASES

The value of real estate properties is determined, in large part, by the leases. As you will recall from earlier chapters, the lease income total is what is capitalized to determine the value of a specific property. Because lease income is so vital to your investment and profit, you need to become an expert on the topic of leases. A good lease protects you, and allows you to collect rent and manage a property in a smooth fashion. A poor lease does the opposite. It does not enforce rent payments, makes it difficult to evict a defaulting tenant, and may create a myriad of other problems. This chapter will provide you with the basics of leases so you can further educate yourself on the subject.

TYPES OF LEASES

There are two general categories of leases — gross and net. With a *gross lease*, the tenant pays only a set amount of rent. The landlord is responsible for payment of taxes, insurance, and other costs associated with the property. With a *net lease*, the tenant pays the rent and a portion of the maintenance fees, insurance premiums, and other operating expenses. When the tenant pays for all fees and operating expenses associated with a space, this is called a *triple-net lease* (or NNN). See Appendix A for an example of this type of lease. This is the type of lease you want to utilize in your investments. At first glance, a triple-net lease may not sound like a good idea for tenants since they pay fees and operating expenses. However, this is not true because the NNN lease allows them to control operating expenses — heating, cooling, electricity, and so on. So, in effect, each tenant in a building pays the appropriate amount for utilities and is not penalized by a poor tenant who wastes a lot of energy by leaving lights, heating, or cooling on all the time. From the investor's point of view, a triple-net lease has several benefits. One, it requires very little or no management. Two, it is low risk. Three, it provides a predictable monthly income from the lease payments. And, four, in some cases you can specify rent increases in the lease agreement to have a hedge against inflation.

THE STRUCTURE OF LEASES

There are thousands of different forms of leases; however, they all have most or all of the following common elements:

- Date of execution

- Lessor's name (landlord)

- Lessee's name (tenant)

- Guarantor's name (if any)

- Amount of rent and date on which it is to be paid

- Start date/end date of lease

- Size and use of premises

- Prohibited activities

- Responsibilities for repairs and maintenance and who pays

- Addresses for legal notices

- Tenant improvement responsibilities

- Liability insurance issues (amount of coverage, who is covered, who pays for coverage, and so on)

- Default or bankruptcy provisions

An example of a commercial lease agreement is shown in Appendix B.

EXHIBITS

The type and number of exhibits will vary with the lease. Often, they include the following:

- Property description (legal description, site plan, floor plan, tenant layouts, and so on)

- Construction specifications, plans, and costs

- Cost of living adjustment/specific rent adjustment (including method of calculation)

- Tenant's acknowledgment of commencement of lease

- Sign regulations

- Estoppel certificate

- Rules and regulations

- Special conditions (any non-standard agreement between the landlord and tenant; e.g., options, exclusives, and so on)

Of course, most of the above will have been worked out during negotiations, except for rules, the commencement document, and the estoppel certificate.

MAJOR LEASE ISSUES

Whatever kinds of leases you deal with, you will find that there are key issues associated with them. This section will acquaint you with seven of the major issues.

Issue 1: The Term of the Lease

The length of a lease can be short-term (month-by-month) or long-term (up to 20 years). Most fall in the mid-range of three-to-five years. Often, the term of a lease will depend on the needs of the tenant. For example, companies that are growing, downsizing, or on shaky ground will most often want short-term leases. That is because they know their space requirements will grow or shrink in relation to their needs. Other, more stable companies prefer long-term leases to avoid the high costs of moving. Or they plan major expenditures on tenant improvements (manufacturing companies, for example). A longer lease also allows tenants to lock in a fixed rental rate and avoid an increase in rent. For the owner, a long-term lease provides security of income over a longer period of time. However, a disadvantage of a long-term lease for owners is that they cannot sell or redevelop the property during that time. They may also have to pay a greater leasing fee to the broker. Finally, they cannot adjust the rent to meet changing market conditions.

Issue 2: The Occupancy Date

Most often, the occupancy date is the same as the lease start date. In some instances, however, a tenant will want early occupancy because they want to set up or make improvements. One problem occurs when the tenant wants free rent during that period. Another problem can occur if the lessor does not have liability and insurance coverage for the occupancy period. So, the lessor should make sure the tenant pays for triple-net expenses and common area expenses during that time. Of course, the lease should include liability and insurance coverage as well.

Issue 3: The Amount of Rent

As you might expect, the rent amount is a significant factor when negotiating any kind of lease. The tenant wants less rent; the lessor wants more. As a lessor, you can reduce objections from potential tenants by quoting a market-based rent. So, as part of the negotiations, you should have available data on comparable spaces or properties. Solid facts and figures show that you have done your research and provide some security to lessees that they are not paying too much for the space or the building. Of course, market surveys can go out the window when the market is rising or falling. When there is a surplus of properties, then lessors compete by lowering rental rates. During a shortage of space, they do the opposite and raise rates because the market will support it. Most leases have rent escalation clauses for inflationary periods. Often, they are tied to the Consumer Price Index. Since no one knows the future, this practice may or not work out for you as an investor. One method to dealing with rises and falls in rent is to keep lease terms short and renegotiate the rent at lease end. For example, if rates are falling but you have a very good tenant you want to keep, you may provide that tenant with special concessions. If the opposite is true — rents are rising and the tenant is unable to find a new location — you can charge premium.

Issue 4: Tenant Improvements

Along with the amount of rent, tenant improvements are often a significant part of lease negotiations. Questions in this area often include:

- What are the improvements?

- Who is to make them?

- How much will they cost?

- Are they general or specific improvements?

- What are the terms of amortization?

- Will the tenant have to remove the improvements at the end of the term?

As the investor, you will favor general improvements because they add to the value and marketability of the property. Single-purpose improvements add little or no value to future tenants. It is common for the lessor to make certain tenant improvements at his or her expense. The lessor can then amortize the cost over the term of the lease and tack it on to the rent.

Issue 5: Options

There are several types of options in leases — the option to buy the property, the option to expand, the option to renew or extend the lease, and so forth. In many instances, the option tends to favor the tenant, so landlords only offer them as a concession. Perhaps the most common is the option to extend the lease term since tenants do not want to incur the expense and hassle of moving to a different property. Less common is the option to expand since it involves alteration of the property's physical structure and may affect other tenants. Least common is the option to purchase since it limits a landlord's flexibility, and lenders do not want a property encumbered by such an option. For both the lessee and the lessor, the main issue in options is the amount of the future rental (or price). As mentioned earlier, landlords certainly do not want to fix a rental price on a property whose value is rising. Renters, on the other hand, want to fix the price for two reasons. If the option price has fallen, they can exercise the option and get a lower rent. If the option price has risen, they can simply defer exercise of the option and negotiate. As an investor, you should be sure to specify during negotiations the length of the option and how much advance notice the renter must give you. For example, if a tenant plans to leave, you want sufficient advance notice (say, six months) in order to find a new tenant and avoid a vacancy.

In terms of option provisions concerning rent, there are several main methods for establishing rent amounts during the leasing period. You may not use all these methods for your leasing purposes, but you should be aware of them.

The first method is *fixed annual increases*. That is, the tenant and landlord agree up front to a specified amount of rent payable over the life of the lease. Here is an example: Assume both parties agree to $5,000 monthly rent on a retail space with a 5 percent yearly increase (not compounded). Now assume the lease is for five years. This means that, in the fifth year, the rent will increase to $6,250 (5 percent of

$5,000 = $250 x 5 years = $1,250 + $5,000 = $6,250). Generally speaking, this method tends to favor the tenant since he or she gets a fixed rent for the lease period and can, therefore, do accurate budgeting. As you might expect, landlords are not as enthusiastic about the fixed-increase method because it, in effect, puts a lid on their income during the lease period. However, the fixed annual increase is one of the most common methods due to its simplicity of calculation and ease of negotiation.

A variation on the above method is fixed *increases at set intervals*. Commonly seen in net-lease investments, these agreements are referred to as "step leases" (or "step-up" or "stepped" leases). Here is an example: Assume a tenant and landlord agree on a ten-year lease. The terms of this lease call for level rent payments for the first five years. Then, at the start of the sixth year, a one-time 10 percent increase kicks in. For the following five years, the rent payments are at this new amount. So, what is the difference between the fixed adjustment and a step lease? In technical terms, the investment is not earning annual compounding rent so the landlord is earning less money on his or her return in the long run.

Another method is the *cost-of-living adjustment* (COLA) approach. As the name suggests, rent is calculated based on changes in accepted indexes, like the U.S. Consumer Price Index or the Wholesale Price Index, depending on the nature of the tenant's business. To calculate a COLA increase, the base rent is adjusted by changes in the U.S. Consumer Price Index throughout the lease term. This method is preferred by landlords since it offers them a measure of protection against inflation. With fixed increases, there is always the possibility that the inflation rate may increase more quickly than the fixed rental rate. When that occurs, the landlord bears the burden of higher property operating expenses. A COLA provision allows the landlord to pass the increases on to his or her tenants, who, in turn, pass additional costs on to their clients or customers. According to the Bureau of Labor Statistics, the national average annual COLA increase has been approximately 2.85 percent throughout the last ten years. See the BLS's site on the Web (**www.ssa.gov/ OACT/COLA/colaseries.html**) for the latest COLA figures. For the tenant, this method has a disadvantage. His or her rent is no longer predictable and, in the worst case, can rise dramatically (from the tenant's point of view). This, in turn, negatively affects the tenant's bottom line. Because of this, the renter and the landlord often agree on limits on COLA increases; e.g., COLA increase not to exceed 5 percent per year.

Another method is the *fair market value approach*. Landlords favor this method since it means they will receive fair market rent and do not have to settle for a lesser amount. Fair market value may be arrived at through appraisals or arbitration. Landlords want the highest and best use of their properties, while tenants want to make sure the fair market value approach does not limit the value of their spaces. Appraisals and, in some instances, arbitration, helps them hash out these differences.

Issue 6: Repair and Maintenance Responsibility

Naturally, tenants do not want to get stuck paying for major repairs (roof damage or replacement, for example). The landlord, on the other hand, does not want to get nickled and dimed to death for minor repairs. In many instances, a 145 compromise is struck during the negotiation of the lease. The landlord is responsible for major repairs and replacement (concealed plumbing, foundations, roofs, and so on). The tenant is responsible for minor repairs, maintenance of HVAC, replacement of broken windows, and so forth.

Issue 7: Subleasing

When a sublease occurs, a tenant (sublessor) leases part or all the premises to another renter (the sublessee). The sublessor is often referred to as the "sandwich" lessor. This is because he or she is sandwiched in between the landlord and the sublessee. Although the sublessor remains responsible for the lease, problems can occur with this arrangement because the sublessee and landlord do not have direct contractual rights with each other or remedies. So, you get questions like: What if the sublessee wants to make improvements? What if the sublessee goes bankrupt? Needless to say, subleasing can unleash a whole torrent of complications, so it is best to consider this area carefully when negotiating a lease.

As you can see from the above issues, it is vital for your financial well-being for you to be fully-versed in all aspects of leases. Ignorance can truly cost you money and cause a lot of headaches. So, always write a good and fair lease, know every detail of that lease, defend it vigorously, and always, always, seek to improve it.

CHAPTER 16

IMPORTANCE OF DUE DILIGENCE

With residential properties, due diligence primarily refers to making sure the home or multi-unit dwelling is in good physical shape. That is not the case with commercial properties. Due diligence has a much broader definition because commercial real estate is much more complicated than dealing with a single-family home or a duplex. It involves not only the physical inspection of the building, but such areas as easements, zoning use, allowed use, encroachments and the like. Effective due diligence is also more necessary in commercial real estate because the consumer protection laws that provide protection in the residential market do not apply in commercial real estate. The law assumes that you are fully knowledgeable about commercial properties when you enter into a contract and so provides fewer remedies in the case of a bad deal.

The purpose of due diligence is, of course, to make sure any land or building you buy or contract you sign is in excellent shape for your investment goals. The flip side of the process is to make sure that you do not buy "a pig in a poke." That is, there are no hidden structural problems or nasty surprises in leases that can come back to bite you in your financial posterior. The degree of due diligence will vary with the complexity of the property under consideration. For example, if you plan to buy raw land or a vacant tract and have no immediate plans for it other than expecting an increase in value over time, due diligence is relatively simple. But if you plan to purchase land and build a strip mall on it, due diligence will need to be much more extensive since you will be dealing with local zoning requirements, the needs of different tenants (parking spaces and such), exits and entrances onto streets or highways, and so on. This chapter will acquaint you with the basic elements of due diligence in the commercial real estate field so you can sail complicated waters and reach the port of financial security with relative ease. As you read through the following material, remember the iron-clad rule of due diligence: *Due Diligence is an absolute necessity and must be done in a thorough and painstaking manner.*

In other words, do not be blinded by the potential profit of an investment and neglect due diligence. And follow the age-old rule: *If it looks too good to be true, most likely it is.* Always apply the "smell test." If there is a whiff of fraud or dishonesty on the part of the seller, back off. You do not want to get involved in legal action. It is time consuming, expensive, and a great way to get ulcers.

So, when should due diligence occur? It takes place before you sign a purchase agreement, of course. And you make clear to all parties from the beginning of the negotiation process that signing is contingent upon the satisfaction of due diligence. Most often, negotiations begin with a *letter of intent.* In the sample letter shown at the end of the chapter, you spell out the fact that due diligence will need to be done and that you will need a reasonable amount of time to conduct all inspections. The other purpose of a letter of intent is to outline your expectations of the deal. How the seller responds will tell you if there is some interest or none at all. If interest is shown, you can then proceed to the next step, which is a *formal purchase agreement.*

The purchase agreement is a legally binding document. **148** Of course, it will be much more detailed and complete than a letter of intent. In terms of due diligence, it will include "subject to" or escape clauses that will allow you to withdraw from the deal *for any reason* if problems are discovered during the review and inspection phase. For example, on the review side, it may be discovered that one party does not have an acceptable credit rating. Or, on the physical side, it may be discovered that a building is not up to code and would require extensive refitting to meet that code. It is wise to assume that the seller has not told you the whole truth about the building, and, therefore, you need to check everything closely. It may be that the seller is unethical. More often, a seller simply may not be aware that a problem exists because they lack the expertise (e.g., hidden plumbing, foundation problems, and the like). In either instance, if you do not conduct proper due diligence, you end up with problems you definitely do not need. During due diligence, you will need the help of specialists to conduct reviews and inspections. The remainder of this chapter deals with areas that need to be analyzed during the process of due diligence.

EASEMENTS

Easements concern the rights of others to pass through or use property. In other words, if parties have easement rights, they can make life difficult for you. For example, you may want to expand parking for businesses only to find that you cannot put in a lot because it interferes with easement rights. Or they may have the right to utility easements (water, gas, electric, telephone) that affect your investment in the property. Easements should be shown on an up-to-date survey, but do not assume they are. Surveyors (or lawyers) can miss items, so it is best to add a level of security by checking with your city public works and building department to make sure nothing has been overlooked.

ENCROACHMENTS

Encroachments are protrusions from another property onto the property you are considering. For example, perhaps the original property line was mis-surveyed, and you find that, say, the next-door building has placed waste bins on it. That is a fairly easy problem to resolve. It gets more complicated when underground installations (septic tanks, fuel tanks, and so forth) are involved. Of course, you would not want potentially hazardous installations on your property, but it is likely you will have to go to court to get the matter resolved and that can cost you thousands of dollars and considerable time. That is why it is important to closely check surveys or to have another survey done.

ENVIRONMENTAL INSPECTIONS

As an investor, the last thing you need is a property that suffers environmental clean-up problems — lead paint, ground water contamination, asbestos insulation, PCBs, and so on. These are extremely expensive problems to fix and can take a considerable amount of time to resolve. And, make no mistake about it: If you buy a property with environmental issues, you are liable for the clean-up. Plus, you cannot re-sell the property easily. That is why such problems are deal-breakers; no one wants the hassle and the cost. If you do decide the deal is worth it, you will need to require that the owner clean up the mess before you purchase the property. In any case, request an environmental report (if one has been done) as part of due diligence. If an analysis has not been done, require the seller to do one so your interests are protected. Also, if you have occasion to have an environmental report done, make sure you hire a certified environmental consultant, contractor, or an attorney who specializes in environmental law. As you might expect, you want them to have considerable experience in their specialty since so much time and money is at stake. Check their references and talk with several of their past or present clients to determine their reputation. If possible, hire a private firm. Government inspectors are available, but then you run into the usual problems with bureaucracy.

CODE VIOLATIONS

Every municipality has building and fire codes that must be met. In some cases, a building may not meet a newer code, but is "grandfathered" in because it met code at the time it was built. Since every town and city operates in different ways, you need to know which municipal department handles specific codes. Of course, the fire department is most likely to handle fire codes, while the building department should be handling building codes, but this is not always the case. So, you will need to dig into local laws and regulations and find which department has the information you need regarding codes. As part of due diligence, you will hire a general building inspection service to inspect the property. Be sure to specify that they should check for code violations because they may not always do that. You do not want the expense of correcting these problems or the expense of a lawsuit if you buy the property and re-sell it in the future and end up with an unhappy buyer.

ZONING

You want to be thoroughly familiar with local zoning uses. If you are not, you could end up not being able to construct the building you want or use the land in a profitable manner. Say you want to build a high-rise apartment building and find out the area is zoned only for low-density multi-family dwellings. You will not be able to go ahead with the project unless you get permission or affect a change in the zoning requirements. Head off such potential problems by knowing exact zoning requirements before entering into a deal.

There is another aspect in relation to zoning that you need to consider and that is "allowed use." Allowed use refers to the fact that the city may allow or restrict a use for a property that is different from zoning requirements. This can be an unpleasant surprise if you do not check closely with the correct municipal departments, especially if use is restricted. If the allowed use is limited and affects future profitability, you can choose not to enter into the deal. Or, if circumstances are right, you can fight city hall to get the use you want.

OTHER ASPECTS OF DUE DILIGENCE

Up to this point, this chapter has dealt mainly with the physical elements of due diligence, but an equally important part of the process is your inspection of the "paperwork" aspect — leases, contracts, and so forth. This section will provide guidelines on that aspect.

Guideline 1: Review All Leases

If you have the experience and the time, you can check all leases closely. However, it is often best to hire a property manager or CPA who specializes in this area. They should either verify that there are no problems or point out areas where potential problems might lie. An *estoppel letter* is the official means of verification. In basic terms, it verifies that the lease attached to the letter is a true and accurate copy of the existing lease and that there are no other agreements between the tenant and the owner. The seller must present the estoppel letter to each tenant and have him or her sign it. That way, if the letter is later found not to be true or accurate, you can file claim against a former tenant, the owner, or both of them.

Guideline 2: Review Inventory Lists

You need to verify that what the seller says is in a building is actually there. So, require him or her to provide you with an inventory list and then visit the property (along with the seller or his representative) to verify that each item is physically present. This can be a time consuming and tedious process, especially with larger properties (e.g., hotels), so you may want to use a property manager or other individual to complete the task for you. Either way, we recommend that you videotape the inspection, which provides visual proof that either an item is present or is missing or that repairs are required.

Guideline 3: Review the Contracts

Depending on the size and complexity of the property, the seller will have several contracts with suppliers — service and maintenance contracts, employment contracts, leased fixtures or goods, insurance agreements, and so on. As a potential buyer, you need to know exactly what these contracts are since you may be responsible for them. If you are unhappy with the prospect of assuming one or more of them, negotiate with the seller during the due diligence period to remedy the matter.

Guideline 4: Obtain a Property Survey

The survey should be recent and certified. A property survey will show the property's legal address — the lot, block, subdivision, and so on, as well as the street address. It will also include the property dimensions and the exact location of any buildings and their outside dimensions. In addition, it should list all utility easements and any deed restrictions. Be sure to compare the survey with the actual property to make sure they match. Because separate teams are involved (title companies, lawyers, banks, surveyors, and so on), it is   153 entirely possible for something to get lost as responsibilities pass from one hand to another. In drastic cases, the survey was done right, but the lawyer sends information on a different property, and the wrong building gets demolished. This can be prevented by making sure the survey matches up exactly with the property in question.

Guideline 5: Validate and Verify All Titles, Liens, and Other Legal Documents

This is a critical area and should be done as early as possible, not left to the last minute. You do not want any doubt whatsoever as to a building being free and clear of unexpected title claimants or unencumbered by debts or liens. If problems do crop up, it is better to take care of them as soon as possible rather than waiting until closing and having an unexpected claim. Hire an experienced title company to go through the title with a fine-toothed comb, since errors and omissions can creep into these documents without anyone noticing. Your attorney should review all other documents in the same manner and provide you with sound and clear advice.

Guideline 6: Set a Due Diligence Timeline

A timeline is usually stipulated in the contract between the buyer and seller. Time can range anywhere from 30 days to 60 days or longer, depending on the size and complexity of the property in question. Often, there is also an extension clause in which the buyer can request more time to complete due diligence. Such a clause is necessary since the seller can be slow in delivering documents or further inspections may be required if potential property problems crop up. Your due diligence timeline should exclude weekends and holidays and stipulate that only business days are part of the timeline. From the buyer's point of view, the longer the due diligence period the better; it gives him or her more time to dig deeper into every aspect of the deal and the property.

Of course, to implement all the above guidelines, you will need to assemble a team; e.g., a building inspector to inspect the property; a title company to review the title; an attorney to review contracts, and so on. You should brief each of them clearly on what you want done so nothing is missed. You may want to put their missions in writing beforehand. This not only will help them out, but will clarify your thinking up front so you will be sure to include every task that needs to be done. Also, make them aware of the due diligence timeline so they will complete their assignments well within the designated period.

Once the team members have completed their assignments, sit down and read the reports carefully. Then, review the reports with each individual; ask questions about areas that are not clear and about any consequences of problems that have been spotted. Do not forget to have each person read the reports of other team members. That way, they get a global view of the property rather than being confined to their own narrow specialty, and they may be able to spot problems that otherwise might have fallen through the cracks.

Often, your team will spot problems because even the best of buildings requires maintenance and repair due to weather and other factors. So, if an inspection reveals physical issues, what do you do? Well, it comes down to the seriousness of the problem. In other words, how much will it cost and how long will it take to fix it? Scraping and painting is relatively inexpensive and does not take much time. Replacing an entire roof on a commercial building is an entirely different kettle of fish. It can be extremely expensive, and you cannot do anything with the building while the roof is being replaced. Of course, if there is a major problem, you have options to deal with it. One, you can have your attorney negotiate with the seller to either fix the problem or lower the price by the amount of the repairs. Two, you can walk away from the deal if the seller refuses to negotiate or will not lower the price enough. Particularly if the seller did not reveal the problem up front, why would you want to deal with him or her, anyway? There may be other hidden issues you do not want to deal with. In cases like this, it is best to simply move on to other, better deals.

SAMPLE LETTER OF INTENT

Mr./Mrs./Ms. Property Owner,

My name is John Jones. I am a local real estate investor, and I have become aware that you are considering the sale of the Oakdale Office Building. I am interested in the purchase of the building and am prepared to pay you $15,000,000 at closing. The closing is contingent upon it occurring within 60 days and approval of my due diligence within a reasonable amount of time. Once property information and date is supplied, the time will be spelled out in the formal agreement.

If I do not approve of reviews and inspections done during due diligence for any reason, I have the option of withdrawing from the contract. Any deposits I place in escrow will be promptly refunded to me as indicated by the terms of the contract.

If the terms above are acceptable, please contact me, and I will have my attorney draft a formal agreement for your review. The agreement document should arrive within five working days after you indicate that the terms are acceptable.

This is a letter of intent and not a formal contract; therefore, no binding purchase agreement will be in effect until we have executed a formal agreement. Once we agree that we will act in good faith in negotiation of the agreement, you agree not to negotiate with any other party for the sale of the property for a period of 30 days. This will allow the formal agreement to be written, reviewed, and executed, if acceptable to both parties.

If I do not hear from you on this proposal by 5 p.m. this coming Friday, this letter of intent shall be considered withdrawn.

Sincerely,

John Jones

Commercial Real Estate Investor

Address, Phone, Fax, E-mail

CHAPTER 17

NEGOTIATING THE PURCHASE AGREEMENT

Purchase agreements spell out how much is to be paid for a property and how that money is to be paid. Beyond that, these agreements also contain contingency clauses that protect your interests. As you might expect, this is one of the most important documents in the entire negotiation process since you are laying your money on the line. So, it is important you write and negotiate the best possible purchase agreement and, at the same time, limit or eliminate as many risks as possible. This chapter will show you how to do that.

DRAFTING THE PURCHASE AGREEMENT

You should draft the initial purchase agreement because you need to know every aspect of the document. See Appendix D for a sample agreement. It is best to write it in plain English. If you are new to commercial real estate purchase agreements and feel you are not a great writer, do not worry. You will get better with practice. Often, a great way to get started is to write a series of simple objectives to guide the writing of the purchase agreement's content. For example:

- To conduct and complete research of the building by July 1.

- To have title examined by June 15.

- To have leases by July 20.

The writing of objectives clarifies your strategy and goals for the deal and, thus, makes it easier to write your drafts of the purchase agreement. Once you are satisfied with your draft, hand it over to your attorney. He or she will "tweak" it so it meets legal standards and covers every contingency. The purchase agreement should parallel your timeline for due diligence and acquisition of the property. In regard to the timeline, be sure every member of your team reviews it so you know all their actions (and yours) can be completed comfortably within that time period.

CONTINGENCIES

As mentioned above, it is important to include contingencies in the purchase agreement to limit or eliminate risks. In any commercial real estate contract, there are standard contingencies. They include in alphabetical order:

- **ALTA (American Land Title Association) survey** — It shows property boundaries, easements, restrictions, and improvements.

- **Estoppel certificates** — If there are any difficulties between the seller and tenants or lender, an estoppel certificate will reveal them.

- **Leases** — These were covered earlier.

- **Loan documents** — They reveal the original cost of the project, as well as allowing you to determine if you want to assume current financing or seek a new financing arrangement.

- **Relevant contracts** — This refers to any contracts the seller has with utilities, service maintenance companies, and the like.

- **Title report and all documents related to the title** — These documents reveal if there are any liens, restrictions, or related encumbrances on the property that could affect your plans for that property.

With any specific deal, there will be other contingencies included in the purchase agreement. Your team will be able to advise you on which "escape clauses" to include. Since contingencies are so important to both parties in a deal, you will need to negotiate them with the seller. He or she will have their own agenda. Your goal should be to arrive at a purchase agreement that makes you both happy. Ideally, once the transaction is completed, you both should agree that it was a fair and equitable deal for all parties concerned. After all, you may want to do business with this person again, and he or she should be happy to do so. Also, smooth negotiations enhance your reputation, and that, in turn, can lead to more business.

How you handle the negotiation of a purchase agreement depends on whether you are the seller or the buyer. If you are a seller, let your broker do the talking. He or she should be an experienced professional who specializes in your area of interest. Your job is to answer questions as they are asked and not talk on and on about the wonders of the property. If you do this, inevitably you will reveal more information than you need to and, in the process, hand the buyer bargaining tools for a lower offer. If you are the buyer, your task is to dig into every aspect of the property. That means you ask as many questions as necessary about the building, the land, the leases, and so forth to obtain as much information as possible. And do not limit your questions to the seller during the due diligence period. Talk to everyone involved with the target property — managers, tenants, lenders, and the like. You want to get as complete a picture as possible and not have everything filtered through the seller's rose-colored glasses.

Depending on the complexity of the deal, the contingency, or "free look," period can range anywhere from about two to six months. During that time (usually the first 30 days), the seller will be required to produce a preliminary title report, the ALTA survey, lease copies, contract copies, and any loan documents. The seller will also need to produce any estoppel certificates during that time. The buyer then has 30 to 60 days to examine all documents. If he or she finds problems, the seller has a month to resolve them. In terms of cost, the seller pays for the documents he or she needs to produce while the buyer pays for the examination of those documents. When closing is achieved, the seller pays the costs for clearing the title (liens and such) and half the cost of the escrow closing. The buyer pays his or her half of the escrow, costs for obtaining financing, and the purchase price for the property (less the paid original deposit).

CHAPTER 18

CLOSING ON A COMMERCIAL REAL ESTATE DEAL

Closing is all about paperwork — your paperwork and the other party's paperwork. If you are a buyer, you have a smaller stack of documents — the initial purchase agreement, a loan application/loan assumption application, and any required approvals. It is all topped off by your signature on the closing document. If you are the seller, you have more documents to bring to the closing. These include the leases, the original loan papers, warranties, accounting documents, copies of contracts in force, service/maintenance agreements, estoppel certificates, a general warranty deed, and formal assignment of leases and contracts that are to remain in force. There are also third-party documents involved, most often from the lender, the tenants, and the title company. These include the preliminary title, commitment/title insurance policy, and loan documents.

From the seller's point of view, the main task is to make sure every document described above is full and complete before the transaction is completed. In terms of leases, any subsequent agreements have to be approved in terms of the planned construction or revamping of a building. Of particular concern are estoppel certificates. As you will recall, an estoppel certificate is a signed statement. Its purpose is to certify that the facts about the property (the lease, rent, expiration date of the lease, and so on) are true as of the date of the statement and can be relied upon by third parties (lender, buyer, and the like). In plainer language, an estoppel certificate certifies that a lease is n force, states the specific rent and terms, certifies that the landlord is not in default, and states the date on which the lease expires. The content of an estoppel certificate will vary the property in question, but the example at the end of this chapter will give you an idea of the typical terms and language. The importance of an estoppel certificate is that lenders and buyers will not execute a deal with it. So, obtaining one is often a necessary but time consuming chore. In addition to estoppel certificates, it is necessary for the buyer to obtain the assignment of leases and warranties, as well as assignment of all lease and utility deposits.

If you are the buyer, your main task in handling all these documents is to closely evaluate their contents and make sure they are accurate and legally sound. But you also have to think long-term. You will need to analyze them to determine whether to keep certain tenants (downsize), the amount of rent to charge, the changing of the leases, and so on For example, you may want to trade current cash flow for a more varied tenant base in order to create stronger income in the future. In this situation, you are aiming more for capital gain than cash flow. In short, the changes you make will depend on your overall financial strategy.

In the end, any deal comes down to money. Keep in mind that, in most instances, the purchase price of any property must be paid in cash. Therefore, you must have money on hand to pay that price. As discussed earlier, most new loans will cover only 75 to 80 percent of the purchase price.

So, as the buyer, you will need cash to pay the remaining amount. The means of acquiring this capital varies with your individual situation. Those with the means can go it alone. Most often, partners are required in order to assemble the required monies. Loans can also be used to pay the balance of the purchase price. An important consideration in terms of a loan is the "cost of funds." This refers to the interest paid, plus points paid. A fundamental example is a simple interest loan. Interest is calculated monthly and is based on the unpaid balance of the loan. An amortization schedule or a debt service constant is used to determine the payment. The debt service constant is figured by a constant percentage times the principle amount. This equation will yield a payment that includes the required annual interest and which provides for complete loan retirement over the life of the loan. The resulting constant is referred to as a "loan constant," and you will find constants in tables or in deal-specific calculations. For example: Assume you have a $100,000 20-year loan with an interest rate of 8 percent and an annual payment of $10,037. You agree to pay back that loan at 10.037 percent of the original loan amount. The constant is figured by this formula:

Annual payment ÷ Loan amount = Constant

So, the calculation for our example looks like this:

$10,037 ÷ $100,000 = 10.037 percent table

The other important factor is the length of the loan. It may include a 25-year amortization rate and a ten-year term. This means the payments are based on a 25-year amortization rate, but the principle balance is due at the end of ten years. This is often referred to as a "balloon" payment. Unlike balloon payments in the residential housing market, this term does not have a negative connotation. For lenders, 163 it is a protection against poor management that allows a property to deteriorate. It also allows them to extend terms if the investment has turned out to be a good one. On the borrower's side, this arrangement can be a good one. He or she can increase loan dollars. This allows him or her to recapture cash equity if the net income before debt service (NIBDS) has been increased to a great degree. This, in turn allows the borrower to tap into capital to improve an existing property or to buy another one while retaining that existing property.

Beyond the cash required to pay the balance of a loan, you also need to consider the fact that you will need a cash reserve to handle any emergencies. For example, you may find that vacancies are higher than expected due to economic or other factors. That means your income will be lower than expected until you fill those vacancies and get rental payments back up to an acceptable level. In the meantime, you will have loan payments to meet so you will need reserve monies to meet those payments. Therefore, from the beginning, you must estimate how much should be in your emergency cash fund. How much will depend on factors like your cash flow, the financial and business condition of the tenants (as well as their size), lease expiration dates, and the like. You may want to accumulate at least six months worth of funds in order to cover the mortgage payments. Or you may want to accumulate it as a percentage of your gross potential income (GPI). Think of your reserve as "peace of mind" money. If the economy temporarily heads south or you have unreliable tenants headed toward vacancies, you will have the comfort of reserve funds to deal with these problems.

CHAPTER 19

MANAGEMENT OF COMMERCIAL REAL ESTATE PROPERTIES

Once you have purchased a property, you begin the work of making it as profitable as possible. There are several elements you must master in order to achieve this objective. This chapter will provide you with an overview of these elements.

PROPERTY MANAGEMENT

If you are new to commercial property management and follow our recommendation of starting small, it would be a wise idea to manage that first property yourself. This will give you an invaluable grounds-eye view of what is involved in taking care of a property on a day-by-day basis. This kind of experience is an investment in your future. That is, as you grow your investment and acquire other properties, you will need to hire property managers since it will no longer make sense for you to take a daily hands-on approach. Therefore, your direct management experience will teach you what to look for in property managers, and you will be able to hire the best person for the job.

Beyond the tenant leases and property management contract,

there are several contractual areas you will need to deal with. Mainly, these concern suppliers and contractors, including:

- Accounting/legal

- Building maintenance (general)

- Building security

- Heating and air conditioning (HVAC) maintenance/ repair

- Insurance

- Janitorial

- Landscaping maintenance

- Leasing

- Parking lot maintenance (snow removal, sweeping, and the like)

- Property management

- Utilities (gas, electric, telecommunications, water)

- Window washing

For now, we will assume that you will be managing a property yourself and handling the above contracts. (We will deal with hiring property managers separately in this chapter.) Based on that assumption, you will contract directly with suppliers. Such contracts should be negotiated on a yearly basis. They should also be severable by each party on short notice. This is important because you definitely do not want a lazy or incompetent supplier or contractor handling services for your property. It can create tenant complaints or even loss of tenants and, thus, loss of income. Most often, one written warning is enough to shape up a contractor since he or she does not want to lose business. However, if a warning does not work, you want the option of getting rid of an under-performing supplier or contractor as quickly as possible. In any contract with a supplier, there are several areas that will need to be addressed. Without exception, any contractor you hire must have insurance in two areas — liability and worker's compensation insurance. If they lack insurance, do not even look at them. It is likely they are a fly-by-night operation at worst or incompetent at best. As a property owner, the last thing you need is expensive liability or worker's comp claims filed against you due to lack of due diligence on your part. Other elements of the contract will include: description of the work to be performed, compensation, hours of operation, exhibits (if any), provisions for severance, and so on. Of course, the contract will need to be signed and dated by both parties.

Utility contracts are of vital importance to your property. If you build a new property, you will handle these contracts yourself so you will know exactly what you are getting and how much it costs. However, if you acquire an existing property, these contracts will already be in place, so it is important to be aware of their details. Utility contracts spell out the services to be provided, the date when they will be available, the type of access to the building, and any physical easements required to route the service into the building. If you are building a new building, you will want the utility companies involved from the very start of the project. After all, these companies typically have many thousands of customers and need lead time in order to schedule the work. Lack of planning on your part can lead to lack of water, power, and the like and some angry tenants. Keep in mind that most utility companies are publicly regulated monopolies. This means you have little leverage with them so it is best to maintain good relations by paying fees early and building enough time into the schedule to accommodate their needs.

Like utilities, insurance is vital to your property investment. That is because they cover liabilities that cost you considerable money if you were not protected against such things as accidents occurring with tenants, workers, or visitors to the building. More detail on insurance is provided in the chapter "The Dull But Vital Top of Insurance," but briefly the types of insurance you will need *during construction* are:

- Fire

- Umbrella (excess liability) insurance — This type of insurance is essential because it protects you against claims above and beyond the amount covered by your primary policies or for claims not currently covered

- Workers' compensation

When you own the building, the types of insurance required are:

- Fire

- Rent replacement insurance (with a worker's compensation rider)

- Umbrella insurance

PROPERTY MANAGERS AND PROPERTY MANAGEMENT AGREEMENTS

You may not want to manage a property yourself, especially if you plan on taking an entrepreneurial path in commercial real estate. The role of an entrepreneur is to grow his or her business, not engage in the day-to-day management of investment properties. That means you will need to hire a property manager. You want the best, most experienced one possible for several important reasons. One, the manager is your spokesperson for the tenants and is responsible for maintaining good relations for them. Two, the manager is the money-handler, collecting rent, preparing budgets, and making rental projections. Three, he or she may handle negotiations with tenants (if you delegate that authority).

The property manager (or you, if you are the manager) will have several important responsibilities. These responsibilities should be spelled out clearly in the manager's contract so he or she can carry out the duties effectively. General duties of property managers are described by the U.S. Bureau of Labor Statistics (**http://www.bls.gov/oco/ocos022.htm**) in this manner:

"...property and real estate managers handle the financial operations of the property, ensuring that rent is collected and that mortgages, taxes, insurance premiums, payroll, and maintenance bills are paid on time."

More specifically, a contract spells out property manager (and owner) responsibilities in most or all of the following areas:

- Accounting

- Advertising

- Clause severability

- Compliance with laws

- Delinquencies

- Equal employment compliance

- Expenses

- "Good Faith" acts

- Handling of creditor claims

- Indemnity (hazardous substances)

- Independent contractor status (stipulates the manager is not an employee of the owner)

- Insurance

- Leasing commissions and renewals (if applicable)

- Lease execution

- Legal proceedings (e.g., arbitration or courts)

- Loan payments (who makes them)

- Maintenance and repair

- Manager compensation

- Miscellaneous charges or fees

- Monthly reports

- Notices (to tenants and others)

- Owner's responsibilities to the manager

- Personnel

- Property's legal description

- Signs

- Successors bound in the event of an assignment

- Supplies

- Taxes

Duties and responsibilities will vary with each contract and may include more (or less) than those listed above.

A WORD ON LEASES

In terms of property management, you have a couple of options in lease handling and execution. You can have a broker handle the leasing or you can have the property manager do it. During property development, a broker will handle leasing arrangements, but once the project is completed, you can go either route. There are advantages and disadvantages to each approach. With a broker, you have a knowledgeable person who is sensitive (or should be) to the market and can find you good tenants. Another advantage is that he or she can be legally prohibited in a continuing contract from stealing your tenants for another project. Once a contract is completed, ethical brokers will not pirate tenants for the simple reason that it can seriously harm their reputations within the commercial real estate community. The alternative is to have your property manager (or the property management company) handle all leasing. The company should offer full sales and leasing services and demonstrate complete, up-to-date knowledge of the market. You may want to offer the property manager a partial commission for finding new tenants to provide an extra incentive for keeping a building fully occupied and your revenue stream flowing. It is good to have healthy and ongoing relationships with property management agencies since their expertise can be invaluable when you decide to sell or expand your holdings.

In Chapter 21, we will cover another important aspect of property management — accounting practices.

CHAPTER 20

MANAGING TENANTS – GOOD & BAD

Once the commercial real estate business is entered, an investor also becomes a property manager — and a manager of people. And that means dealing with all the good and bad traits of individuals. Let us look at good tenants first.

MANAGING GOOD TENANTS

Tenants are customers, and, as in any business, they should be treated well. It is not only the right thing to do; it also makes good business sense. After all, they are sources of the best kind of advertising — word-of-mouth. They will help spread an investor's reputation among their families, friends, and business associates. It does not have to be expensive to create and maintain good will with good tenants. As always, communication is the key. Send them birthday cards, holiday cards, etc. Phone them to make sure everything is going well in their lives and with the property. And, although they should have been made responsible for maintenance in the contract, it never hurts to lend a helping hand; for example, mentioning good places to get bargains on paint, drapes, etc. This will help them save money while getting the benefit of an improved property. All in all, treat good tenants well and considerable rewards will be reaped in terms of good will, less hassle, and more word-of-mouth advertising.

MANAGING BAD TENANTS

In the real estate business, it is likely that a tenant who is late with payments, misses payments, does not maintain the property, or who disappears will be encountered. The best way to avoid this, of course, is to qualify applicants carefully up front. It is proof of the old adage, "An ounce of prevention is worth a pound of cure." However, if a bad tenant slips through, then apply the steps described below.

Step 1: Try to work things out over the phone or in person.

Call or visit the tenant to pin down what the problem is. Sometimes, a tenant is experiencing financial difficulties through no fault of their own, has shown good faith in the past, and is committed to paying. In a case like this, consider accepting a partial payment and take the risk that they may not be able to pay. It is a matter of judgment. However, if excuses of "the dog ate my homework" variety start occurring, then this should set off some alarms. These are usually excuses similar to "My aunt/grandfather/cousin died," "I lost my paycheck," "I didn't get paid." In cases like this and when payments are consistently late or missed, it is obvious that the second step needs to be taken.

Step 2: Notify the tenant in writing of eviction.

If calls or visits did not rectify the situation, then it is time for eviction. This is a last resort, of course. Before this step, the investor should have stayed in reasonably close touch with the tenant so he or she has a feel for a reality of the situation. As mentioned above, some tenants are good people with unexpected problems. Others will flat out lie and have plenty of excuses.

No one likes to evict tenants; however, it is paramount to remember that landlords have a duty to take care of themselves and their investors. Money is being lost when the tenant does not pay. Eviction is not an easy or pleasant process, but a landlord can safeguard himself or herself from the start by making sure the contract has been worded so that it is subject to the rental agreement being followed. It can be wording similar to this: "This contract will be declared null and void if any rental payment is made ten days or more late." The wording adds additional written legal underpinning for beginning the eviction process and provides the landlord with another layer of protection. To notify the tenant of eviction, be sure to send the letter via U.S. certified mail, return reply requested. In the letter, state clearly why the eviction proceedings have been instituted and attach a copy of the option agreement with the appropriate sections highlighted.

If legal steps needed to be taken to collect past due amounts, check with the state's regulations. They vary from state to state. For example, in some states, as a landlord, wages, bank accounts, state tax refunds, etc. can be garnished. In other states, the garnishment route cannot be taken. Another course to take is to employ the services of a collection agency, but their services are not cheap. They may take anywhere from 40 to 60 percent of the amount recovered.

An intermediate step before eviction is suggested by Matthew S. Chan in his book, *TurnKey Investing with Lease-* 175

Options. He recommends the "sign and leave" approach because he wants to avoid eviction whenever possible. It is a time consuming and costly step and, in his opinion, the last resort. He points out that up to 30-45 days of rental income can be lost from the time the eviction notice is filed until he gets legal possession of the property. In effect, Chan's "sign and leave" policy asks the tenant to relinquish legal possession of the property in exchange for not filing an eviction notice. It allows the tenant the opportunity to get out of the lease and leave peacefully. Chan then negotiates a settlement amount or lets the tenant go, depending on the amount owed. Be sure to check with a real estate attorney to see if this approach complies with the state's real property laws.

MORE DETAIL ON THE EVICTION PROCESS

Be sure to protect lease option investments in every way possible. It makes sense to acquire as much knowledge about evictions as possible — as unpleasant as the subject may be. Here are more details on the process so an investor can become knowledgeable on the subject and protect his or her lease option investments.

In legal terms, eviction is also known as *possession, unlawful detainer, forcible detainer*, or a *summary proceeding*. Basically, an eviction is a lawsuit to get a court order to remove a tenant. Remember, by law, a tenant cannot physically be removed from the premises. No matter how obnoxious the tenant has been, do not take steps like the following:

- Using or threatening to use force

- Interrupting or discontinuing essential services

- Removing the occupants' possessions from the dwelling

- Removing the entrance door

- Removing, plugging, or rendering inoperable the entrance door lock

- Changing the lock on the entrance door without supplying the occupant with a key

Before commencing with the proceeding, the tenancy must be terminated. This is done by serving notice on the tenant as required by the state law. The notice is typically three to five days for non-payment of rent. After that time period, court proceedings can begin if the tenant has not paid the rent in full or moved out. The informal proceedings, much like a small claims court, can range from ten to 30 days.

Upon issuing a "judgment" or "order" in the landlord's favor, the court issues a legal document called a "warrant" or "writ". The warrant orders the appropriate enforcement agent to forcibly remove the tenant from the premises. The agent normally changes the locks and removes the personal property of the tenant. These days, few tenants are actually thrown out. Check with the county officials to see if the landlord is required to hire movers and store tenant property. Be sure to become familiar with landlord-tenant laws in the county; however, we do not recommend pursuing evictions before a court unless a person is also an attorney. Hire an attorney to do the job. And, do not hire just any attorney; hire one who specializes in the area of landlord-tenant law. To get practical advice at the ground level on dealing with evictions, talk to other experienced landlords in the city or town. They will be able to provide good hands-on advice. If there is a landlord's association in the area, join it and gain access to the combined knowledge of its members.

Another method of dealing with evictions is advocated by attorney, entrepreneur and speaker, William Bronchick (**http://www.reiclub.com/authors/Bill%20Bronchick. html**). He points out that evictions take time. In other words, the longer the defaulting tenant is in possession of the property, the more money can be lost. His strategy is to offer the tenant cash to leave right away. Although this may seem counterintuitive, Bronchick points out that it makes good financial sense. He argues, if the matter can be settled quickly without going to court, do it. Of course, do not rely on the tenant's promise to move and pay him or her before they leave the property. Instead, wait until they vacate, clean the property, hand over the keys, and sign a written release of liability.

Bronchick also points out the need to deal with the security deposit, whether the tenant leaves voluntarily or by legal force. Security deposits are subject to state law whether or not a landlord is entitled to them. The rules are approximately the same in most states: the security deposit has to be returned within 30 days or a certified letter has to be sent to the tenant telling him or her of the reasons why it is being kept. Even if the landlord is entitled to retain the deposit, failure to follow the proper procedure will result in a lawsuit for improper withholding. Remember, the tenant can be sued in small claims court for rent owed and damages to the property; however, the landlord cannot withhold the security deposit without following the rules.

CHAPTER 21

ACCOUNTING PRACTICES FOR COMMERCIAL REAL ESTATE PROPERTIES

We assume that you are familiar with basic accounting practices since you are interested in commercial real estate investments. If you are not, you need to gain a thorough knowledge of accounting practices before proceeding with the buying and selling of properties. The numbers in these documents provide you with absolutely vital information. This chapter will acquaint you with the basics of accounting as it relates to real estate.

ACCOUNTING TOOLS

The tools you will be using include formal accounting reports, bookkeeping, and spreadsheets. These applications are available in computerized accounting packages, which make the whole process much easier and cheaper. Let us look at each of these tools in more detail

Accounting

Double-entry bookkeeping is a standard, uniform system of tracking financial data. The "double-entry" term refers to the fact that there is a debit and credit side to any transaction. So, when individuals (an accountant, for example) look at a ledger, they should see a balance between the two sides. Here is a basic example: Assume you have $1,500 of rental income from a tenant. On one side of the ledger, this is entered as such. On the other side, it is entered as cash in the bank. An accountant can quickly scan the ledger to see if there is a balance or if errors have occurred. If errors appear, he or she has to correct them and achieve a correct balance.

All this information can be used to generate a number of useful reports — earnings statements, financial statements, and comparison reports (on a monthly or yearly basis). Essentially, these reports provide a complete "bird's-eye" view of the financial health (or lack of it) of your investment. They are also required to report income to the Internal Revenue Service. Financial documents include balance sheets, income statements and cash flow statements. Let us look briefly at each of these statements in turn so you can understand their importance in maintaining and improving financial health.

THE BALANCE SHEET

The balance sheet is one of the most important financial documents to pay attention to. As you can see at the end of the chapter, it summarizes a company's assets, liabilities, and shareholder's equity at a specific time. At a glance, you can see what you own (assets), what you owe (liabilities), and the specific and total equity. In short, you (and investors) get a snapshot of the state of your financial health. It is known as a balance sheet for accounting reasons. By definition, the balance sheet must be equal or in balance. In the simplest form, assets must equal liabilities, or assets must equal

liabilities plus equity as shown in the following formula:

Assets = Liabilities + Equity

In the Assets section, each type of asset is listed. *Assets* are any item of economic value that you or your investors own. On a balance sheet, assets are arranged in order of liquidity; that is, how quickly they can be turned into cash. So, naturally "cash" is listed first and includes cash-on-hand and in the bank. Assets are divided into "current" and "fixed.

In corporate and other balance sheets, *current assets* include cash, accounts receivable, securities, inventory, prepaid expenses, and anything else that can be converted into cash in one year or during the normal course of business. "Hard" and "soft" costs can be included under current assets. Hard costs refer to the direct costs necessary to construct a building (labor, material, equipment, and so on). They are also known as "brick and mortar" costs. Soft costs refer to those items in a project necessary to prepare and complete the non-construction needs of that particular project. They include such items as architecture, consultants, design, engineering, environmental studies, inspections, permits, and so forth.

Fixed assets are assets that produce revenue. They are also called "long-term" assets because they are not intended to be sold. Fixed assets can include such items as office furniture, vehicles, real property, building improvements, and machinery and equipment. The depreciation on fixed assets should be deducted from the asset values to prevent overvaluation.

Other assets are generally fixed assets that are intangible. In commercial real estate, this can include refundable deposits and the like. (In other business areas, other assets can include patents, royalty arrangements, copyrights, goodwill, life insurance on officers and key employees, and so on).

Depending on the situation, intangibles are sometimes not included on a balance sheet because of the difficulty of valuing them.

Total assets are the sum total of both current and fixed assets (plus any other "miscellaneous" assets like refundable deposits and the like).

Liabilities are your debts. Like assets, they are divided into two categories — current and long-term. Liabilities should be arranged on the balance sheet in order of how soon they must be repaid. For example, payroll taxes and sales taxes might be listed first because they must be paid within 30 days, while notes payable are usually due within 90 days to a year. Depending on the type, loans may be due over a period of months or years, while mortgages may have 30 year terms.

Current liabilities include accounts payable, notes payable, accrued expenses, such as wages and salaries, taxes payable, and the portion of long-term debts due within one year from the date of the balance sheet. They are summed up in the Total Current Liabilities column.

Long-term liabilities are any debts that must be repaid more than one year from the date of the balance sheet. They may include start-up financing or mortgages. All liabilities are totaled in the line item Total Liabilities.

Equity is the ownership in your properties. It can include your ownership and the ownership of members if you have taken on partners for your commercial real estate properties. The sum of ownership is totaled in the Total Member Equity column.

THE INCOME STATEMENT

The income statement goes hand in hand with a balance sheet. As you can see in the example at the end of the chapter, it shows how much revenue and profit your investment has generated over a certain period. Together, these two documents present a complete picture of your finances.

SPREADSHEETS

Spreadsheets provide a "ground's-eye" view of rental income, lease expirations, and expenses. In other words, they tell you what is happening with your property on a short-term basis (weekly, monthly, and so on). Spreadsheets take different forms. One may give you the breakdown of your monthly expenses. Another tells your income from rent; e.g., it tells you who has paid their rent and who has not. Yet another will allow you to do projections so you can increase your income at a rate that will grow your investment on a reasonable basis.

As mentioned earlier, there are many software applications that will generate these financial reports for you. However, you may want to create your own so you can include details pertinent to your specific property. A "generic" computer form may not allow you to do that.

SAMPLE BALANCE SHEET (CASH BASIS)	
December 31, 2007	
Assets	
Current Assets	
Cash (Smith Bank)	1,645.23
Total Current Assets	1,645.23
Construction in Progress: Building 1	0.00

SAMPLE BALANCE SHEET (CASH BASIS)	
Total Land & Building	0.00
Total Soft Costs	0.00
Total Hard Costs	0.00
Total Costs: Building 1	0.00
Building 2	
Total Land	0.00
Soft Costs	0.00
Total Soft Costs	0.00
Hard Costs	0.00
Total Hard Costs	0.00
Total Building 2	0.00
Fixed Assets	
Office Equipment & Furniture	2,111.46
Machinery & Equipment	0.00
Accumulated Depreciation: Mach & Equip.	0.00
Total Fixed Costs	2,111.46
Other Assets	
Deposits: Refundable	2,190.55
Organization Expenses	195.00
Suspense (an account that is used on a temporary basis for receipts, disbursements, or discrepancies)	-291.99
Total Other Assets	2,183.75
Total Assets	5,940.44
Liabilities	
Current Liabilities	
Payroll Taxes Payable	0.00
Sales Tax Payable	-8,760.45
Total Current Liabilities	-8,760.45
Total Liabilities	-8,760.45
Equity	
Partner's Equity	
Partner 1	70,015.89
Partner 2	15,015,89

SAMPLE BALANCE SHEET (CASH BASIS)	
Partner 3	15,015.89
Partner 4	-98,123.50
Partner 5	-99,001.01
Partner 6	111,777.73
Total Partner Equity	14,700.89
Liabilities & Equity	**5,940.44**

SAMPLE STANDARD INCOME STATEMENT	
XYZ Company 1/1/2007 to 12/31/2007	
Revenue	
Operating Revenue	
Contracting Income	422,036.45
Rental Income	0.00
Total Rental Revenue	0.00
Interest & Finance Charge Income	535.36
Total Revenue	422,571.81
Expenses	
Costs & Expenses	
Bank Charges	121.32
Building Rent	2,444.00
Contracting Costs	295,111.10
General/Administrative Expenses	121.32
Insurance & Bonds	2,655.00
Insurance: General	-599.62
Legal & Accounting	710.45
Office Supplies & Postage, etc.	130.23
Operating Supplies	145.66
Permits & Fees	375.11
Telephone	807.26
Total Expense	302,021.83
Net Income	120,549.98

CHAPTER 22

THE DULL BUT VITAL TOPIC OF INSURANCE

Insurance is not one of the most exciting aspects of commercial real estate investment, but coverage is absolutely essential to have in order to protect your investments. So, spend time on this chapter to understand the basics of coverage. That way, you will be well-protected on every project you undertake. In general terms, commercial real estate insurance is divided into two categories — coverage during construction and coverage as an owner managing a building.

COURSE OF CONSTRUCTION (BUILDERS RISK) INSURANCE

There are many risks inherent in a building project whether it is large or small. Therefore, the right "course of construction" or "builders risk" insurance is vital for you to cover those risks and prevent potentially devastating financial losses. As the name indicates, this insurance covers buildings and other structures while they are being built. It includes building materials and equipment that is intended to become part of the building or structure. The coverage applies to property while at the job site, off site in storage, and in transit. Construction equipment coverage (i.e., bulldozers, forklifts, and so on) is provided by the contractor's equipment insurance.

On a typical project, there are several parties to a construction contract — the project owner, architects/ engineers, general contractor/subcontractors, lenders, and so forth. Each of these parties has insurable interests in the overall construction project. For example, equipment and materials are often on or off the job site, which means that, at different times, they may belong to the owner, general contractor, or subcontractors. If each of the parties involved dealt separately with insurance, gaps in coverage could occur. Therefore, one party often takes on the responsibility for insuring the project on behalf of all the other parties. That responsibility is spelled out in the construction contract.

Insurance requirements in the construction contract may be spelled out in standard documents published by professional organizations (e.g., the American Institute of Architects or the Associated General Contractors). However, as an owner, you may want to combine your own specific insurance requirements with the standard forms. Generally speaking, the following elements of insurance will be included in the contract:

- "All-risk" coverage

- Coverage for material that is stored off-site and in transit

- Coverage for all parties to the contract (owner, contractors, subcontractors, and so on)

- Permission for waivers of subrogation* among the parties

- Coverage for the duration of the project

*"Subrogation" is defined as the taking on of the legal rights of someone whose debts or expenses have been paid. Subrogation is used by insurers to acquire from the injured party rights to sue so they can sue to recover any claims they have paid.

As the project owner, you can add the construction project to your regular commercial property policy, or you can buy separate builders risk coverage.

Our recommendation is to buy separate coverage because it has a couple of distinct benefits. For one thing, coverage is much broader than that provided in standard commercial property insurance; it may include flood, earthquake, and testing, as well as provide broader transit and off-premises coverage. For another, course of construction policies usually contain fewer exclusions. One potential disadvantage is that you have to get permanent coverage in place once the builders risk policy expires. In other words, you can create problems for yourself if you are not aware of the date when the course of construction policy lapses and creates a gap in coverage. Of course, due diligence on your part will prevent occurrence of such a situation.

As an owner, you also have the option of delegating the responsibility for buying builders risk coverage to a general contractor rather than purchasing it yourself. This is an advantage on larger projects because general contractors are likely to be more knowledgeable on the subject than you are. They may also prefer to have more control over the selection of the project insurer. This arrangement is fairly common in the industry. If you decide to go this route, be sure to let the general contractor know in writing before the project starts.

BUILDING OPERATION INSURANCE

Of course, once a building is completed, you want to protect yourself and your investment against as many contingencies as possible. Below, we have listed the most common types of insurance to have. Depending on the type of building and the area where you live, you may not need them all. However, you should be familiar with each type.

BOILER AND MACHINERY INSURANCE

Boiler explosions can have horrendous consequences for the person who is the victim of such an accident and result in expensive claims against you. We once met a maintenance man who had caught the full force of a boiler explosion. His chest and arms were horribly scarred. He required extensive skin grafts and a long recovery period. Beyond the basic fact that you want the victim to get good treatment, you also do not want to get stuck with the bill for such expensive medical procedures. Of course, such insurance should not cover only boilers but also heavy machinery, pressure tanks, large compressors, heavy air conditioners, and the like. A plus for this type of insurance is that the insurer often becomes a partner with you in the sense that they seek to keep losses to a minimum by regularly inspecting the equipment to make sure it is well-maintained and operating safely.

EARTHQUAKE INSURANCE

If your projects lie in an earthquake zone, you may want

this insurance. It is relatively expensive (relative to other insurance policies), but cheap compared to the damage a quake can inflict in just a few seconds. One caution: When you choose an insurer, be sure that the insurer has considerable assets and will not be wiped out by extensive damage across its coverage area. Note: An earthquake policy is always a separate policy and is not covered under extended policies (see below).

EXTENDED COVERAGE INSURANCE

In addition to fire insurance (mentioned below), consider extended or "comprehensive" coverage, which covers damage caused by such events as aircraft accidents, burst pipes, collapse, explosions, falling trees, hail, landslides, rioting, vandalism, water discharge (accidental), and so on.

FIRE INSURANCE

Carry this coverage for loss of or damage to a building and/ or contents due to fire. Remember that your building should gain in appreciation and value, so make sure your property is covered with a policy large enough to pay current replacement costs. Also, do not let insurance companies try to oversell you on fire insurance, but, by the same token, do not try to save money on premiums by going too cheap on coverage.

FLOOD INSURANCE

Like earthquake insurance, flood insurance is always a separate policy. It covers damage caused not only by flooding, but high water or sewage backups (or should). Due diligence can keep you from buying or building in areas that are flood prone. Or it can help you calculate the probability of flood occurring so you can judge the risk.

LIABILITY INSURANCE

With liability insurance, you protect yourself against potentially expensive lawsuits for such various events as wrongful eviction claims, negligence accusations, discrimination, and the like. Our advice is to buy insurance that will cover you against the widest range of liabilities and get the highest limits possible (if you do not have umbrella insurance as described below).

RENT REPLACEMENT INSURANCE

Carry this insurance to insure that your income stream from a lease is not interrupted due to fire or some other mishap. If you do not have this coverage, you will end up paying for fixed expenses out of your own pocket. With rent replacement insurance, the insurance company will compensate you for your loss over a reasonable period of time while the building is being repaired. The premium is a small price to pay to head off consequences that could devastate your finances.

UMBRELLA LIABILITY INSURANCE

Commercial umbrella ("excess") liability insurance is an important source of protection that supplements the limits of your underlying policies — general liability, automobile liability, employer's liability, and so on). Such a policy also protects you from exclusions and gaps that exist in your primary liability insurance. It is sold in increments of $1 million and provides valuable coverage for large projects like commercial real estate investments. In its simplest form, it works like this: Assume you have an auto insurance policy with liability limits of $300,000 and a homeowner's policy with a limit of $250,000. With $1 million umbrella, your limits become, in effect, $1,300,000 on the auto policy and $1,250,000 on a homeowner's liability claim. A vital point to remember about an umbrella liability policy is that it holds you accountable for maintaining the policies listed in the schedule of underlying insurance. During the term of the umbrella liability policy, they must be kept in force without alteration of any of the terms and conditions.

WORKER'S COMPENSATION INSURANCE

If you have employees at your building, absolutely have this insurance. Medical bills for on-the-job injuries can be astronomical these days, so the premiums are a cheap alternative to paying these claims. Most states require employers to have coverage for their employees. The rates vary, but they are often reasonable and are based on a percentage of workers' earnings and the type of work they do. In general, the greater the risk at work, the higher the percentage. Be sure to classify your workers correctly since insurers conduct periodic audits to ensure you are paying the right premiums. If possible, try to get coverage through a group rather than an individual insurer. Group rates are cheaper. If you have multiple properties, buy a single policy that covers workers at all the buildings, then divide the costs up among the properties when you pay the bill.

Select only the kinds of coverage you require for your type of building and for your location. In addition, do careful calculations to determine the amount of coverage required so you do not end up under- or over-insuring the property. Also, it is wise to shop around for coverage to get the best coverage for the best rates on a regular basis before renewal dates arrive. Rates change, and you may be able to find a better deal. Another alternative is to hire an insurance consultant to review your properties and coverage to make recommendations for reducing premium costs.

CHAPTER 23

THE SALE OF COMMERCIAL REAL ESTATE PROPERTIES

Up to this point, we have discussed the building, acquisition, and management of properties. As you grow your holdings, however, there will come a time when you want to sell a property. You may simply want to get the profit from that investment, or you may want to use the sale money to invest in other, more valuable properties. Whatever your objective, you want to get maximum profit from the sale.

The first step to getting a maximum profit is relatively simple — have a building that is in optimum shape so you can "dazzle" prospective buyers with its potential. A shoddy, poorly maintained building is not going to attract anyone and certainly is not going to get you the greatest money from a sale. It also will not get you the broadest range of buyers. A well-maintained property, on the other hand, is easier to sell because buyers can see they will not get saddled with repair and maintenance costs. They will also see that tenants are happy and, therefore, the potential income stream will remain high.

The second step is to be able to provide interested buyers with proof of the value of the property. This can be provided in a current spreadsheet on operating costs. Simply put, you can show buyers hard-and-fast figures to justify the price you are charging for the property. For example, if you can show interested parties that leases will automatically increase in the next year, you have demonstrated the great potential of the building. Remember, leases are where the income stream comes from. If an investor sees happy tenants, full occupancy, and escalating rents, he or she will more likely agree to your sales terms.

Of course, any sale is a process of negotiation as you learned earlier from the position of the buyer. This means you will run into objections from interested investors. It is a natural part of the sales process. The best way to handle objections is to be prepared to handle them. Think of the specific objections you had as a buyer and what answers sellers gave you that satisfied those objections. You can then practice handling them by yourself or with a friend or business associate. You cannot anticipate every possible objection, but practice will allow you to handle them more smoothly and effectively. There is another way to handle objections or prevent them from coming up in the first place — a sales presentation that "wows" prospective buyers.

OVERVIEW OF THE SALES PRESENTATION

Any good sales presentation is a combination of persuasion and hard facts. It is best to be as visually and verbally professional as possible. Essentially, you want to tell a story about the property that excites prospective buyers. And you want to tell one that makes your property stand out from any other investments a buyer may be considering. With today's software (PowerPoint and the like), you can

create a compelling presentation by yourself at a low cost. If you are new to making presentations, the key is to practice thoroughly ahead of time.

A primary element of your presentation will be the building itself and its history. You want to show the building as it was when you bought it, as well as its current physical and financial condition. This will require a combination of photographs and the original spreadsheet information on tenants. The presentation will be extremely effective if you can demonstrate the improvements (financially and physically) that have taken place since you assumed ownership.

Another important element is your projections for the future. Any buyer wants to see the potential in a purchase. Support your projections by basing them on current, solid leases. The lease numbers should include the following:

- **Cash flow** — This can be on a monthly, quarterly, or yearly historical basis. Buyers will probably prefer a monthly basis since it is the most current.

- **Expense history** — Also on an historical basis.

- **Initial and current tenant information** — In spreadsheet format.

- **Income and operating cost history** — Only in relation to the net income before debt service (NIBDS) and expense numbers relevant to the proposed sale. Other information is none of the buyer's business. To ensure privacy in this respect, require that a non-disclosure agreement be signed by the buyer before any numbers are discussed.

One important aspect of the sales presentation that we have

not mentioned yet actually occurs before the presentation — qualifying the buyer. By qualifying, we do not mean financial qualifying (although that is certainly part of the process). We mean selling the right property to the right buyer. For example, if you have a small office building for sale, you probably would not want to pitch it to a large investor or an REIT. It is likely they would be more interested in mid-size to large office buildings, so you would end up wasting your time and theirs. A better target audience would be an individual investor. So, zero in on the appropriate audience right from the start of the sales process.

SALES PRESENTATION DETAILS

A presentation can be made by you or by a property investment broker. If you are new or lack confidence, use a broker. If you do it yourself, it will be cheaper since brokers charge a fee for this service. With a broker, you can be sure the sales presentation will be done professionally. It is also likely that the property will sell faster since the broker will be better known in the investment community. One method of reducing a broker's commission is to negotiate a long-term relationship with him or her. They should be willing to do this since it provides them with future business. Another option is to allow the broker to invest his or her commission with you at the time of the sale. This is called a "carried commission." The benefit for brokers is that they can earn a good return on the investment when the property is sold. However, if the broker is with a large brokerage house and not independent, it is likely that carried commissions will not be allowed. On the positive side, such large firms often permit lower commissions, saving you money. In the end, the choice of making a presentation yourself or using a broker is dependent on your individual needs and sales presentation skills.

As mentioned earlier in this chapter, it is best to be as visual as possible in a sales presentation. In fact, it is absolutely vital since buyers will want to see what the proposed construction will look like or what an existing building looks like. Here are the visuals that should be part of any sales presentation:

- **Photos** — These will present existing buildings and should be professionally done, not "snapshots" taken by amateurs. You want the building to be presented in as attractive manner as possible. Often, an aerial photograph of the property is also included.

- **Renderings** — Drawings are used to present future construction and have the same purpose as photos — presenting an attractive package. They are also used with existing buildings to show location of the property in relation to the city and highways. In terms of new construction, two additional renderings will be required — an overall site plan and initial floor plans. During the due diligence period, you will need to provide detailed floor plans that include specifications, plans of existing tenant improvements, and so on. The last drawings will be the "as-built" plans. These renderings show all changes made to the original blueprints. Often, they show the building location, easement locations, buried utilities, and the location of any additional structures or installations.

Of course, all the photos and renderings sell the "sizzle" of your property. The numbers sell the "steak" and are what any investor will take a hard look at. Those numbers should be accurate and up to date, and projected income and   199 expenses should be realistic. Your spreadsheet information will provide the following accounting information for interested investors:

- GPI (gross potential income)

- Actual vacancy rate

- EGI (effective gross income)

- Total operating expenses/operating expenses recovered from tenants

- NOI (net operating income)

- Property management fees (if any)

- NIBDS (net income before debt service)

- Debt service

- Cash flow

- Increased/decreased percentage on an annual basis over the first year shown on the spreadsheet

Be aware that buyers will have done studies during the due diligence period to determine the value of your property in comparison with similar properties on the market. If you have done an excellent job of maintaining your property and increasing its value, you have a right to ask for a higher-than-market value. In this situation, let your property speak for itself. Do not run down the competition when the buyer brings up the market study. It is unprofessional and may, in fact, harm your presentation since no one likes to deal with negative people. At this point, you may be wondering how to price your property correctly before you even get to the sales presentation. We will cover that subject next.

PRICING THE PROPERTY

The first step in pricing your property is to determine market conditions. You will need to ask yourself questions like: "Is it the right time to sell?" "How is my market segment doing right now?" "What's the overall condition of the local economy?" In effect, instead of completing due diligence for purchase of a property, you are completing it for a sale. That is, you are carefully checking every aspect of prevailing conditions to see if the time is right. Common sense tells you that the best time to sell is in a time of good employment and a rising economic tide. It also tells you that the worst time to sell is when unemployment is up due to poor economic conditions. A good source for all this information is the brokerages in your community. They can provide you with the data needed to make comparisons with other properties in your target market and let you know what the prospects are for a sale in the current economic climate.

Let us assume the conditions are right, and you are ready to sell your property. To get the profit you deserve, you will need to price it above the market average. Again, if you have maintained the building in excellent condition and can demonstrate its present and potential profit with solid facts and figures, this should not be a difficult task. A price that is anywhere from 10 to 15 percent above average is realistic. The range may be higher or lower, depending on local conditions and the quality of your property in physical and financial terms.

To set a price, first look at the competition. Check to see what prices other buildings in your specific market are getting for leases. Of course, know the specific types of leases (gross or net) so you are comparing apples to apples. If you can offer triple net (NNN) leases while others are offering gross leases, you are in the driver's seat. NNN leases are much more attractive to buyers so you can command a better sale price. This also relates to net income before debt service (NIBDS). In other words, if you can demonstrate a strong and increasing cash flow from the property, that property becomes significantly more attractive to a potential buyer, and, again, you can command a higher sales price. Finally, a good strategy is to check your asking price with a lender to see if it is realistic in terms of current conditions. He or she will be willing to provide you with that information since it may mean future business for them. You may even consider applying for financing with that lender on behalf of prospective buyers. It saves time. And not only that, it is a big plus for your sales presentation because buyers will be impressed that financing is, for all practical purposes, immediately available due to your professional management of the property and demonstrated income results.

Once you have all the above elements in place, make sure the building is in tip-top shape. Although, as mentioned earlier, leases are the important part of the sale, the condition of the building itself is physical proof to potential buyers that they would be buying a good investment. So, make sure all maintenance is up to date, the grounds are in good order, and the building exterior is as attractive as possible. Next, select a time to sell. As mentioned earlier, choose an "up market" when buyers are more plentiful and have money to invest. If the market is down, keep the building for a better time.

If the market is right, your next step is to prepare a sales document. It should be timed to the due diligence period. In other words, you want to be able to assemble all necessary documents during that 30-day period so you can deliver them as soon as possible after escrow opens. Earlier in this book, we pointed out that estoppel certificates are the real time-eaters. So, pay close attention to their execution and delivery during the due diligence period so unwanted delays do not occur. And do not forget any residual guarantees or verbal side agreements with tenants. You must make the buyer aware of them since most of these agreements are honored after the sale. Disclose them in writing and have them acknowledged by all parties involved.

In the end, you will have a smooth and successful sale if you do all your homework and prepare a thorough presentation.

CHAPTER 24

THE MARKETING OF COMMERCIAL REAL ESTATE PROPERTIES

Marketing of commercial real estate properties is not that much different from the marketing of any other product — you have to get the word out about that property. Plus, you want to present it in the most attractive way possible to get the best price. This chapter provides you with an overview of the most common and effective methods of marketing and advertising your properties. Remember that you will most likely need to use a mix of methods. These days, there is so much advertising and marketing "noise" out there that it may be hard for potential buyers to hear your message. The best marketing is targeted. Particularly in the commercial real estate area, a "shotgun" approach is a waste of time and money. You are appealing to a limited and knowledgeable audience (in relation to residential properties, anyway) with specific investment goals and objectives. Depending on the size of your property, most of your marketing efforts may be directed at brokers to make them aware that you have a good investment for sale. However, investors often drive areas and neighborhoods to see what is available in the market, so you also want to make your property's availability visible to others. You can do that with combination of the following methods.

COMMERCIAL MULTIPLE LISTING SERVICES (MLS)

Without a doubt, this is one of the most effective methods of marketing a property. Brokers consult Internet-based MLS listings regularly because they are a great source of current information on properties. They exchange information with other brokers and search for properties for their clients. In general, the listings allow users to specify exactly what they are looking for — size, location, property type, price, and so on. A list of targeted properties can then be generated, saving time and aggravation.

Commercial MLS services come in a variety of sizes and shapes. They can be local or national, privately owned, or run by an association. Some are fee-based and some are free. In general, a subscriber service is worth the money because it is more targeted and more likely to have up-to-date facts and figures. The best ones offer a wide menu of other services, including:

- Lender information

- Mortgage information

- Market information

- Broadcast e-mails/fax services

- Appraisal data

- Property information

Here is an example of how you can use an MLS service: Assume you have an industrial property you want to sell. Using the service, you can enter prospect requirements and then have your property information broadcast to brokers who specialize in industrial properties. Be aware that there is a downside to this technique, however. You may get unqualified prospects responding to your message or vendors wanting to sell you services and products you have no interest in. It is also a possibility that other owners will contact you seeking competitive information.

PERSONAL CONTACTS

As you grow your business, you will be building a network of contacts. They will be an excellent source for both sales and purchases of properties. Depending on your area of specialty, contacts can range from brokers to utilities to banks to someone you simply become acquainted with at a local Chamber of Commerce meeting. So, it is wise to develop your network right from the start and continue to maintain and expand it throughout your career.

NEWS RELEASES

While you most likely will not use a news release to directly promote the sale of a building, this is still an excellent (and free) way to promote your name and keep it in front of interested prospects. Investors read the business section to keep up on the latest deals and other information. Once they read about you, they will do some research and find out that you have a property to sell. Most local newspapers are happy to print your news release. Be sure to send the information to the appropriate editor. If you really want to establish and promote your name, contribute articles on real estate to the newspaper on a regular basis. This gives you status as an expert.

BROCHURES

You should prepare a brochure for every property you sell. Brochures allow you to present a property in an attractive and professional way. A good brochure catches the eye with beautiful visuals and compelling content. Of course, it should contain the vital details on the property you want to sell, for example:

- Property description

- Photo of property

- Location

- Physical details

- Terms of lease or sale

- Zoning

The amount of detail you provide in a brochure will vary with the property you have for sale. Our advice is to have a professional do the brochure so it makes a great first impression on everyone who receives it. Not only do you want the brochure to say, "This is a great potential investment," you also want it to reflect your professionalism. Poorly designed brochures say the opposite and turn prospects (and brokers) off. So, spend the time and money to get all your brochures done well and correctly.

SIGNS

Signs are your 24-hour-a-day advertising tool. They attract the attention of everyone passing by your property. More importantly, they attract the attention of prospects and brokers who often like to check out properties they are interested in. Like brochures, signs should be professionally done to present an equally professional image. They can be of any size, shape, and construction. The size can range from a window sign to 6' x 8' or larger, depending on the nature of the property. Any sign should list the pertinent information — for sale, your name, the company name, telephone number, and so on. Of course, your sign should be placed in the most visible place possible so you will get the greatest number of views. Once you make a sale, be sure to slap a SOLD sticker on the sign to promote your success.

DIRECT MAIL

This method is not as important as it once was due to the impact of the Internet. However, it may have a place in the promotion of yourself and any property you have to sell or buy. The good thing about a letter and an accompanying brochure is that they cannot be deleted like e-mails (or blocked by spam filters). Once a broker or prospect has a physical piece of attractive paper in his or her hands, he or she is more likely to read the information. For mailings to be effective, they should be carefully targeted to your intended audience and area of specialization; e.g. industrial, retail, and so forth. For example, if you have an industrial property for sale, you could try direct mailings to local manufacturers. Or, if you have a professional office building for sale, you could mail to service groups who might be interested in the purchase of such a property.

ADVERTISING

Since most prospects and brokers interested in commercial real estate do not look to the newspaper classifieds, radio, or television for information on the subject, this is not 209 a particularly apt method of moving a property. Media advertising probably gives you the least bang for your buck in comparison to the methods described above. However, it does have its place in terms of self-promotion. If you want to make your name known to the community, you can use advertising to announce completed deals, provide testimonials, or just promote yourself and your company.

CHAPTER 25

THE SUBJECT OF TAXES

One of the greatest advantages of commercial real estate investment is the tax benefits. Such investments allow you to legally shelter income and defer capital gains. In effect, you can minimize taxation and maximize the money you keep on an after-tax basis. But you can only take advantage of these benefits if you thoroughly understand the tax laws and keep current on them (they tend to change relatively often). This chapter will discuss the basics of real estate tax advantages so you have a working knowledge of them. However, the best way to stay on top of the laws is to hire an experienced accountant or tax advisor who is a specialist in your area of interest.

DEPRECIATION

The first advantage of commercial real estate investment is *depreciation*. In the tax code, it is now called "cost recovery." Cost recovery assumes that assets (buildings and the like) will lose an equal amount of value each year due to wear and tear. It is a "non-cash expense." In other words, it does not actually take cash out of your pocket; instead, it is treated as an expense or deduction when totaling up your income. Depreciation allows you to decrease your taxable income which, in turn, lets you shelter positive cash flow from taxation.

The net effect of depreciation is that it lowers income taxes for the current year and defers them to a later date. *Defer* is the key word. Do not make the mistake of thinking depreciation will eliminate income taxes; it will not. In technical terms, an annual depreciation deduction is figured on a *reduction in basis* of the rental property. This is calculated as your original cost in the property plus capital improvements. This is then *recaptured* (added to your taxable profit) in full and taxed upon the sale or disposition of your property. Be aware that land itself is not depreciable. After all, unlike buildings, land does not wear out. So, if you want to enjoy larger depreciation benefits, make improvements to your buildings.

Under present tax laws, *straight-line depreciation* is used for recently acquired rental properties. This form of depreciation uses a method of calculating the depreciation of a property which assumes that property will lose an equal amount of value each year. The annual depreciation is calculated by subtracting the *salvage value* (the estimated value of the property at the end of its useful life) of the asset from the purchase price, and then dividing this number by the estimated useful life of the property. The *recovery period* is the period of time during which the depreciation is taken. The IRS has specific rules for straight-line depreciation for commercial properties. The recovery period is 39 years (or an annual cost recovery of 2.564 percent). The IRS classifies mixed-use properties as commercial unless the income from the residential portion is 80 percent or more of the gross rental income.

CAPITAL GAINS

This income is generated when investments (real estate, stocks, and so on) are sold for a profit. Any income you realize from a sale is subject to taxation as a capital gain. Capital gains are classified as:

- **Short-term:** Any property held for 12 months or less. The capital gains are taxed at the same rate as ordinary income.

- **Long-term:** Any property held longer than 12 months. The capital gains are taxed at lower rates than ordinary income. Currently, the maximum long-term gain rate is 15 percent.

To determine what part of your income will be taxed (and how), you will need to complete a cash flow analysis in order to determine the positive or negative cash flow from a property. The analysis of cash flow statements can get complicated; however, below is the basic formula used:

Rental Income
-_____Expenses*
Net Taxable Income

Net Taxable Income
x_____Tax Rate
Tax Liability

Operating expenses, debt service interest, capital improvement expenses, damages, theft, and rental income depreciation.

TAX DEFERRED EXCHANGES

Another great advantage of real estate investment is the *Tax-Deferred 1031 Exchange* law. A detailed explanation of this concept is provided in Appendix C. However, here is a basic explanation: The 1031 exchange permits you to sell one property and buy another without incurring capital gains taxes. You simply have to re-invest all your profits into the next property (or properties) within a specific timeline. A 1031 is a good long-tem strategy because it allows you to keep expanding your portfolio and your wealth while legally delaying the payment of taxes. Keep in mind that the properties in a 1031 exchange must be "qualifying property." This is defined as property held for investment purposes or used in a taxpayer's trade or business. Investment property includes improved or unimproved real estate held for investment or income producing purposes. Real estate must be replaced with like-kind real estate. Improved real estate can be replaced with unimproved real estate and vice versa. Here are some examples of regulations in that regard:

- A 100 percent interest can be exchanged for an undivided percentage interest with multiple owners and vice-versa.

- One property can be exchanged for two or more properties.

- Two or more properties can be exchanged for one replacement property.

- Investment property can be exchanged for business property and vice versa.

By law, you cannot exchange a personal residence for income property, and income or investment property cannot be exchanged for a personal residence, which you will reside in. There are three types of 1031 tax deferred exchanges that can take place:

- **Straight exchanges** — Two parties trade properties of equal or approximate value.

- **Multi-party exchange** — It involves three or more parties buying, selling, or exchanging properties. These exchanges tend to be complex, and you will definitely need a tax professional to guide you through the process.

- **Delayed exchange** — This method allows the sale of the relinquished property and the buying of the replacement property to occur at different times as long as stringent rules are followed. This is the exchange most often used.

Below are some basic rules that must be followed in order to qualify for a 1031 exchange:

- The properties to be exchanged must be located in the United States. (You can exchange foreign property for foreign property and domestic for domestic. However, you cannot mix these exchanges together.)

- You must trade only like-kind real estate.

- An exchange must be made that is equal to or greater than in value and equity. Any cash or debt relief received above this amount is considered "boot" and is taxable. For an explanation of the concept of "boot," read the information in Appendix E.

- The like-kind property must be identified within 45 days of the closing on the initial property.

- All proceeds from the initial sale must be turned over to a "qualified intermediary" (QI, facilitator, exchanger), who is the person or company that plays the role of middleman. Any of the proceeds not under the control of the middleman are subject to taxation. **215**

The middleman holds the funds from the initial property in escrow until such time as the closing on the second property occurs. The middleman also assists the owner with the preparation of paperwork and other services to ensure the transaction progresses smoothly.

- The closing on the second property must take place within 180 days following the close on the first property.

As stated earlier, the 1031 exchange option is a good way to achieve long-term growth and income. It is part of the "wealth-building" strategy advocated by Gary Keller in his book, *The Millionaire Real Estate Investor* (recommended reading). So, if you would like to build an extensive commercial real estate portfolio, you should definitely take advantage of 1031. However, be aware that this option has its minor limitations. For one thing, you have to re-invest all your proceeds (including the original investment and your profit) into the new property. Second, as stated above, you have a limited amount of time in which to identify the exchange properties and arrange for the exchange of those properties. Third, suitable exchange properties are not always easy to find. That is why you need the services of a professional to broker and facilitate the process. You will also need the services of an attorney who specializes in this area. As you might expect, there is a lot of paperwork involved in exchanges and much of it has to do with the Internal Revenue Service. So, it all has to be done right. If it is not, there is the possibility the exchange might not be approved, and you will end up having to pay taxes you did not anticipate.

APPENDIX A

TRIPLE NET COMMERCIAL LEASE

Article of Agreement made on _____(date) between _____
_____ (name and address of landlord), hereafter referred to as
"Landlord," and _____ (name and address of
tenant), hereafter referred to as "Tenant."

It should be know that the Landlord is the owner of the property located at _____
_____ in the township of _____ in the county of _____
_____. Hereafter, this property will be referred to as the "Leasehold
Premises."

It should be known that the Tenant wishes to rent and lease the Leasehold Premises
and that the Landlord and the Tenant have reached an agreement based upon the
following terms and conditions.

This agreement is legally binding; the Tenant shall pay all rents herein discussed, and
the Landlord shall lease the property to the Tenant, while adhering to the following
guidelines:

1. Term: This Lease shall be in effect for _____ years and _____ months
   and shall begin on _____ (date) and shall end on _____
   _____ (date).

2. Rent: The Tenant shall pay the Landlord _____ (amount in
   dollars and cents) on _____ (rental due date) each and every
   month that the Tenant occupies the Leasehold Premises.

3. Security Deposit: In addition, the Tenant shall also pay the Landlord a security
   deposit in the amount of _____ before the Tenant uses or occupies
   the Leasehold Premises. This deposit will be held as security for any damages, costs,
   or expenses incurred to the Leasehold Premises while the Tenant is occupying

TRIPLE NET COMMERCIAL LEASE

the Leasehold Premises. Unless the Landlord intends to withhold the deposit, the amount shall be returned, whether in part or in whole, to the Tenant within 30 days after termination of this lease.

4. Utilities: During the term of this lease, the Tenant shall pay all utility bills for the Leasehold Premises, including the gas, electric, telephone, cable, water, sewer, and garbage collection, as well as any service charges pertaining to these utilities.

5. Clean and Sanitary Condition: While occupying the Leasehold Premises, it is the Tenant's duty to keep and maintain the Leasehold Premises and the surrounding area in a clean and sanitary condition. This includes keeping the area free of garbage and debris, which shall be deposited in the proper garbage collection containers, for which the Tenant is responsible for placing curbside for pickup and moving once pickup has occurred. The Tenant is responsible for any fines incurred due to not keeping the Leasehold Premises in a clean and sanitary condition.

6. Maintenance: It is the Tenant's responsibility to keep and maintain the Leasehold Premises in good condition at all times. The Tenant shall abide by the rules and regulations set forth by the health officer, fire marshal, building inspector, and any other property officials. All costs pertaining to the keeping and maintaining of the Leasehold Premises are the responsibility of the Tenant, even if the Tenant neglects doing so. In such a case, the Landlord may make the repairs and charge the costs to the Tenant. When the lease expires, the Tenant must surrender the Leasehold Premises in good condition, with reasonable amounts of wear and tear.

7. Liability Insurance: The tenant shall have a policy of public liability and property damage insurance for the Leasehold Premises. These amounts shall not be less than _____ for injury or death to one person in an accident, _____ _____ for injury or death for an occurrence, and _____ for property damage for an occurrence. The insurance policy shall list the Landlord and Tenant as the insured and shall also include a clause stating that the insurer will not make any changes to the policy without first notifying the Landlord in writing 30 days prior to doing so. The insurance company must be approved by the Landlord and the Landlord shall be given a copy of the policy.

8. Personal Property Insurance: The Tenant agrees to carry insurance for all fixtures, furnishings, equipment, and any other personal property located on

TRIPLE NET COMMERCIAL LEASE

or in the Leasehold Premises. This insurance shall be no less than 100 percent of the replacement cost of the property. The Tenant must provide the Landlord with a copy of this policy.

9. Off-Set Statement: The Tenant agrees to provide the Landlord with a written statement confirming a) that this lease is in effect, b) that the commencement date stated above is correct, c) that the rent has been paid in advance, and d) if the lease has been modified, and identifying any changes. The Landlord must verify that these statements are valid.

10. Attornment: If the Leasehold Premises are brought for foreclosure, the Tenant shall attorn to and agrees to recognize the successor as the new Landlord under this lease.

11. Subordination: The Tenant agrees that this lease is secondary to any mortgages or deeds of trust that may be placed on the Leasehold Premises. Any advances, interest, renewals, replacements, and extensions will be recognized by the Tenant if there is a foreclosure if the Tenant is not in default.

12. Assignment and Subletting: The Tenant cannot assign or transfer the Lease without the written consent of the Landlord. The Tenant cannot sublet the Leasehold Properties or any part of the property without written consent from the Landlord. If the Tenant chooses to assign or sublet the Leasehold Premises, the Landlord will not lose any rights as assigned in this lease. Additionally, the Tenant will in no way be released from the provisions in this lease if the Tenant does choose to assign or sublet the Leasehold Premises.

13. Waste or Nuisance: The Tenant is prohibited from leaving waste on the Leasehold Premises and from placing any load on the floor that is greater than the floor load per square foot area. The Tenant also will not use or permit the use of anything that may be a nuisance.

14. Reconstruction of Damaged Premises: If the Leasehold Premises are damaged by fire, whether in part or in whole, and the property is no longer inhabitable, the damages will be immediately repaid. However, the Landlord may choose not to rebuild; as such, the minimum rental and other charges, as they are in proportion to the damaged property, will cease. The Landlord will not be required to repair or replace the Tenant's fixtures, furnishings, or personal property. If more than 25 percent of the Leasehold Premises is damaged, the Landlord may choose to end the lease but must give the Tenant written notice of this decision within 90 days of the damage.

TRIPLE NET COMMERCIAL LEASE

15. Total Condemnation of Leased Premises: If the Leasehold Premises is acquired by any public authority, the lease will cease on the day the public authority takes possession of the property. The Tenant is responsible for paying the rent up to that day, and the Landlord must present the Tenant with a refund for any rent that was paid in advance.

16. Partial Condemnation: If the whole property is not acquired by a public authority but more than 25 percent is taken, the Landlord has the right to end the lease or to restore part of the Leasehold Premises to the complete unit. If the Landlord chooses to do the latter, the lease and all terms herein established will remain in effect; however, the rent must be reduced in proportion to the amount of the Leasehold Premises seized.

17. Landlord's and Tenant's Damages: Any damages awarded in part or in whole to the Leasehold Premises when it is seized by a public authority are the property of the Landlord in whatever form the award is in. The Tenant does not have any claim to these awards.

18. Default: All rights of the Landlord discusses here are cumulative and do not exclude any other rights given by law. The tenant agrees that:

    a. If the Tenant does not pay any portion of the rent at any time or for any reason and remains in default for ten days;

    b. If the Tenant leaves the property or fails to keep the Leasehold Premises open for business each day or fails to uphold any parts of the lease for a period of ten days or more; if the Tenant is found to be in default the Landlord has the right to enter the property, whether the Tenant or a third party is occupying it; if the Landlord must go to court to collect the due fees, the Tenant must compensate the Landlord for any fees pertaining to collection, including attorney's fees up to 10 percent or $500, whichever is greater.

19. Right of Entry: The Landlord has the right to enter the Leasehold Premises at any reasonable times to inspect and make repairs, alterations, improvements, or additions as necessary or as desired. While the repairs are being done, the Tenant is not responsible for paying rent if the Tenant is unable to occupy the Leasehold Premises while said repairs are being completed.

20. Loss and Damage to Tenant's Property: The Landlord is not responsible for any loss or damage to the Leasehold Premises due to any loss or damages caused

TRIPLE NET COMMERCIAL LEASE

by the adjoining tenants. This includes the bursting or leaking of any water, gas, sewer, or steam pipes.

21. Notice by Tenant: The Tenant must notify the Landlord immediately if there is a fire in the building or if an accident has occurred in the building or on the premises as a result of any defects, fixtures, or equipment belonging to the Leasehold Premises.

22. Holding Over: Any holding over after the lease expires will be on a month by month basis at a minimum rental amount of _____.

23. Successors: All rights given to the Tenant and the Landlord, as outlined in this lease, extends to the heirs, executors, administrators, successors, and assigns of the Tenant and the Landlord. If there is more than one Tenant, they are both bound by the terms of this lease.

24. Landlord's Covenant: If the Tenant pays the rent and observes the terms outlined in this line, the Tenant will be able to peacefully and quietly hold and enjoy the Leasehold Premises for the entire rental term without being hindered or interrupted by the Landlord or any party acting on the part of the Landlord.

25. The Buyer, _____ (name) has the option to purchase the Leasehold Premises from the Seller, _____ (name). The Seller will pay the Buyer _____ (amount) for this option. The receipt of this sale must be recognized by the Buyer and the Buyer's heirs, successors, assigns, or representatives. The receipt of this sale gives the Buyer the right to the property located at _____
(street address), with the following terms and conditions:

   a. Option Period: This option begins on _____ (date and time).

   b. Exercise: The Buyer may exercise this option at any time during the Option Period by providing the Seller with a written notice that the Buyer wishes to exercise the option.

   c. Contract Upon Exercise: When this option is exercised, the Buyer must complete a standard agreement to purchase real estate.

   d. Application of Option Money: In the event that this option is exercised, the option money __will __ will not go toward the purchase price at closing.

TRIPLE NET COMMERCIAL LEASE

26. Waiver: If the Landlord chooses to waive any part of this lease, this does not mean any subsequent breaches will be waived. The Tenant must obtain permission from the Landlord prior to committing a similar act. Only waivers signed by the Landlord will be accepted.

27. Notices: Any notice, demand, or request surrounding this lease must be sent by United States certified mail with a return receipt requested, postage prepaid, and addressed to the Landlord or the Tenant at their specified addresses.

28. Recording: The Tenant may not record this lease without the Landlord's written consent. If the Landlord grants this request, a short form of this lease may be made for recordation. The short form must include descriptions of the parties involved, the Leasehold Premises, the lease terms, and any special provisions.

29. Transfer of Landlord's Interest: If the Landlord transfers his or her interest in the Leasehold Premises, the party to whom the interest was transferred is relieved from any obligations beginning with the date of transfer. This includes the security deposit.

30. Accord and Satisfaction: If the Tenant pays the Landlord a lesser amount than the agreed upon rent, this money will be viewed as a payment toward the rent.

31. Entire Agreement: This lease and its contents contain all the agreements made between the Tenant and the Landlord concerning the Leasehold Premises. The Tenant and the Landlord have not made any other agreements, be they verbal or written, concerning this property. No changes may be made to this lease unless the Tenant and the Landlord sign and approve it.

32. New Taxes: The Tenant will be responsible for any taxes levied by the government in any form.

33. Heirs and Successors: This lease is binding and passes to the parties' heirs, successors, representatives, and assigns.

34. Counterparts: The Tenant and the Landlord may sign this lease in one or more counterparts, and each counterpart will be combined into one agreement. This lease is valid if the signatures are executed by facsimile.

WITNESS: LANDLORD:

_____   _____

WITNESS: TENANT:

_____   _____

APPENDIX B

COMMERCIAL LEASE FORM

Dated _____

This Lease is made by and between _____
_____ (referred to as "Landlord") and _____
_____ (referred to as "Tenant"). In consideration of the
mutual promises, covenants, agreements, and conditions contained herein and for
other good and valuable consideration, receipt of which is hereby acknowledged,
the Landlord and Tenant agree to the following:

1. The Landlord is hereby leasing to the Tenant the premises located at _____
    _____, and the Tenant is now renting said property from
    the Landlord. The premises is described as:_____
    _____ _____
    _____.

2. The Lease term, beginning _____ (date), and ending _____
    _____ (date) is for _____number of months.

3. Tenant agrees to pay Landlord rent in the amount of $_____ per year,
    payable in equal monthly installments of $ _____.

4. This Lease is subject to all mortgages, whether present or future, affecting
    property described above.

5. Tenant may use and inhabit said premises only as a _____
    _____ (Tenant Rental Status) and is at all times subject to approval of the
    Landlord.

6. The Tenant is prohibited from making any alterations, additions, or improvements
    to said property without first receiving written consent of the Landlord.

COMMERCIAL LEASE FORM

7. The Landlord, at his own expense, will provide following utilities or amenities for the Tenant's use and benefit: _____
_____
_____

8. The Tenant, at his own expense, agrees to provide the following:
_____
_____
_____
_____

9. The Tenant is required to purchase, at his own expense, public liability insurance in the amount of $ _____ as well purchasing fire and hazard insurance in the amount of $ _____ for the property and is must provide Landlord satisfactory evidence of purchase of said insurances and must keep insurance policies in force and effect during entire life of Lease.

10. The Tenant is prohibited from permitting or committing waste on said premises.

11. The Tenant is required to abide by and comply with all rules, regulations, ordinances codes, and laws of all governmental authorities who have jurisdiction over said property.

12. The Tenant prohibited from being involved in, or allowing, any activity which will impose an insurance increase for the building and/or property in which the premises is contained Tenant is also prohibited from committing or permitting and nuisance to said building or property.

13. The Tenant shall not sublet or assign the premises nor allow any other person or business to use or occupy the premises without the prior written consent of the Landlord, which consent may not be unreasonably withheld.

14. At the end of Lease, Tenant must surrender and relinquish said property in the same condition (subject to any additions, maintenance, alterations, or improvements, if any) as property presently exists in (excluding reasonable wear and tear).

15. If Tenant defaults on any term or condition provided in this Lease, the Landlord is permitted the right to undertake any or all other remedies as permitted by Law.

COMMERCIAL LEASE FORM

16. This Lease is hereby binding, and inure to the benefit of the parties as well as their heirs, successors, and assigns.

Signed this _____ day of _____ (Month) _____ (Year).

_____

Tenant's Printed Name

_____

Tenant's Signature

_____

Landlord's Printed Name

_____

Landlord's Signature

APPENDIX C

1031. EXCHANGE OF PROPERTY HELD FOR PRODUCTIVE USE OR INVESTMENT

(a) Nonrecognition of gain or loss from exchanges solely in kind

(1) In general

No gain or loss shall be recognized on the exchange of property held for productive use in a trade or business or for investment if such property is exchanged solely for property of like kind which is to be held either for productive use in a trade or business or for investment.

(2) Exception

This subsection shall not apply to any exchange of—

    (A) stock in trade or other property held primarily for sale,

    (B) stocks, bonds, or notes,

    (C) other securities or evidences of indebtedness or interest,

    (D) interests in a partnership,

    (E) certificates of trust or beneficial interests, or

    (F) chooses in action.

For purposes of this section, an interest in a partnership which has in effect a valid election under section 761 (a) to be excluded from the application of all of subchapter K shall be treated as an interest in each of the assets of such partnership and not as an interest in a partnership.

(3) Requirement that property be identified and that exchange be completed not more than 180 days after transfer of exchanged property.

For purposes of this subsection, any property received by the taxpayer shall be treated as property which is not like-kind property if—

    (A) such property is not identified as property to be received in the exchange on or before the day which is 45 days after the date on which the taxpayer transfers the property relinquished in the exchange, or

(B) such property is received after the earlier of—

(i) the day which is 180 days after the date on which the taxpayer transfers the property relinquished in the exchange, or

(ii) the due date (determined with regard to extension) for the transferor's return of the tax imposed by this chapter for the taxable year in which the transfer of the relinquished property occurs.

(b) Gain from exchanges not solely in kind

If an exchange would be within the provisions of subsection (a), of section 1035(a), of section 1036(a), or of section 1037(a), if it were not for the fact that the property received in exchange consists not only of property permitted by such provisions to be received without the recognition of gain, but also of other property or money, then the gain, if any, to the recipient shall be recognized, but in an amount not in excess of the sum of such money and the fair market value of such other property.

(c) Loss from exchanges not solely in kind

If an exchange would be within the provisions of subsection (a), of section 1035(a), of section 1036(a), or of section 1037(a), if it were not for the fact that the property received in exchange consists not only of property permitted by such provisions to be received without the recognition of gain or loss, but also of other property or money, then no loss from the exchange shall be recognized.

(d) Basis

If property was acquired on an exchange described in this section, section 1035 (a), section 1036(a), or section 1037 (a), then the basis shall be the same as that of the property exchanged, decreased in the amount of any money received by the taxpayer and increased in the amount of gain or decreased in the amount of loss to the taxpayer that was recognized on such exchange. If the property so acquired consisted in part of the type of property permitted by this section, section 1035 (a), section 1036(a), or section 1037 (a), to be received without the recognition of gain or loss, and in part of other property, the basis provided in this subsection shall be allocated between the properties (other than money) received, and for the purpose of the allocation there shall be assigned to such other property an amount equivalent to its fair market value at the date of the exchange. For purposes of this section, section 1035 (a), and section 1036 (a), where as part of the consideration to the taxpayer another party to the exchange assumed (as determined under section 357 (d)) a liability of the taxpayer, such assumption shall be considered as money received by the taxpayer on the exchange.

(e) Exchanges of livestock of different sexes

For purposes of this section, livestock of different sexes are not property of a like kind.

(f) Special rules for exchanges between related persons

(1) In general

If—

(A) a taxpayer exchanges property with a related person,

(B) there is nonrecognition of gain or loss to the taxpayer under this section with respect to the exchange of such property (determined without regard to this subsection), and

(C) before the date 2 years after the date of the last transfer which was part of such exchange—

(i) the related person disposes of such property, or

(ii) the taxpayer disposes of the property received in the exchange from the related person which was of like kind to the property transferred by the taxpayer, there shall be no nonrecognition of gain or loss under this section to the taxpayer with respect to such exchange; except that any gain or loss recognized by the taxpayer by reason of this subsection shall be taken into account as of the date on which the disposition referred to in subparagraph (C) occurs.

(2) Certain dispositions not taken into account

For purposes of paragraph (1)(C), there shall not be taken into account any disposition—

(A) after the earlier of the death of the taxpayer or the death of the related person,

(B) in a compulsory or involuntary conversion (within the meaning of section 1033) if the exchange occurred before the threat or imminence of such conversion, or

(C) with respect to which it is established to the satisfaction of the Secretary that neither the exchange nor such disposition had as one of its principal purposes the avoidance of Federal income tax.

(3) Related person

For purposes of this subsection, the term "related person" means any person bearing a relationship to the taxpayer described in section 267 (b) or 707 (b)(1).

(4) Treatment of certain transactions

This section shall not apply to any exchange which is part of a transaction (or series of transactions) structured to avoid the purposes of this subsection.

(g) Special rule where substantial diminution of risk

(1) In general

If paragraph (2) applies to any property for any period, the running of the period set forth in subsection (f)(1)(C) with respect to such property shall be suspended during such period.

(2) Property to which subsection applies

This paragraph shall apply to any property for any period during which the holder's risk of loss with respect to the property is substantially diminished by—

(A) the holding of a put with respect to such property,

(B) the holding by another person of a right to acquire such property, or

(C) a short sale or any other transaction.

(h) Special rules for foreign real and personal property

For purposes of this section—

(1) Real property

Real property located in the United States and real property located outside the United States are not property of a like kind.

(2) Personal property

(A) In general

Personal property used predominantly within the United States and personal property used predominantly outside the United States are not property of a like kind.

(B) Predominant use

Except as provided in subparagraphs (C) and (D), the predominant use of any property shall be determined based on—

(i) in the case of the property relinquished in the exchange, the 2-year period ending on the date of such relinquishment, and

(ii) in the case of the property acquired in the exchange, the 2-year period beginning on the date of such acquisition.

(C) Property held for less than 2 years

Except in the case of an exchange which is part of a transaction (or series of transactions) structured to avoid the purposes of this subsection—

(i) only the periods the property was held by the person relinquishing the property (or any related person) shall be taken into account under subparagraph (B)(i), and

(ii) only the periods the property was held by the person acquiring the property (or any related person) shall be taken into account under subparagraph (B)(ii).

(D) Special rule for certain property

Property described in any subparagraph of section 168 (g)(4) shall be treated as used predominantly in the United States

APPENDIX D

AGREEMENT FOR SALE OF COMMERCIAL REAL ESTATE

Date:

This Agreement, by and between _____ and _____
_____, of _____ (Address), now referred to
as the "Seller(s)," and _____ and _____
__, of _____ (Address), now referred to as the
"Buyer(s)", In consideration of the mutual promises, covenants, agreements, and
conditions contained herein and for other good and valuable consideration, receipt
of which is hereby acknowledged, the Buyer(s) and Seller(s) agree to the following:

1. The Sellers are agreeing to sell to Buyers and Buyers are agreeing to purchase
   the land and buildings located in _____ Township, _____
   __ County, and _____ State which is/are described in Deed to Sellers
   recorded in _____ County Record Book _____, on Page _____. The
   aforementioned property contains _____ acres, more or less.

2. The agreed upon price of purchase price is $_____. The Sellers
   hereby acknowledge Deposit in the amount of $_____ due prior to the
   signing of this Agreement. Deposit will be held by _____
   until closing has been completed, and will then be considered a credit toward
   the amount owed on the total purchase price.

3. Allocations. Seller(s) and Buyer(s) agree that the Purchase Price is to be
   allocated as described below, and that allocations provided below are fair and
   reasonable and are the result of negotiations between both parties for the
   terms and conditions of this sale:

AGREEMENT FOR SALE OF COMMERCIAL REAL ESTATE

Personal Property, Equipment & Fixtures $_____

Buildings $_____

Land $_____

Total $_____

4.   Each Party is required to pay one-half of the _____ (State) and __ _____ (Local) Realty Transfer Taxes due. Each side's payment is expected to be $_____ .

5.   The real estate taxes for the dates __/__/20__ to __/__/20__ are to be prorated beginning the date of closing, with the Township and County taxes to be prorated on a calendar-year basis, and School tax to be prorated on a fiscal-year basis. Possession of said property will be transferred at closing.

6.   Seller is responsible for and holds all risk of any losses from fire or other casualty until closing.

7.   Seller(s) is/ are prohibited from leaving waste on property and must maintain the property and land in-like condition until closing. Buyer(s), prior to closing, are permitted the right to inspect the property and land as long as a forty-eight (48) hour written notice is submitted to the attorney of the Seller(s).

8.   Appliances: The following appliances are to be conveyed with the property and are required to be in good working order at the time of closing. Any appliances found to be in need of repair must be repaired by Seller(s) prior to closing, or the cost of said repairs will be deducted at closing. List of Appliances: _____

_____

_____ .

9.   The Buyers are hereby notified that the premises described in this Agreement are not serviced by a community sewage treatment facility, but require an on-site septic system. Buyers should contact the local agency charged with enforcement of the Pennsylvania Sewage Facilities Act to learn the requirements prior to signing this Agreement.

10.   To the Seller(s) knowledge, as of the date of closing, Seller(s) represent and warrant the following to the Buyer(s):

a.   Seller(s) are not, nor is the property, in violation of any law, environmental statute, ordinance, regulation, requirement, or directive of any kind;

b.   Said property is not subject to any zoning regulation; and

AGREEMENT FOR SALE OF COMMERCIAL REAL ESTATE

c.   Said property is not the subject of any lawsuit.

11.   The Seller(s) hereby certify that, to the best of their knowledge, understanding, and information, there have not been any hazardous substances dumped on the property by any person, firm, or entity. Seller(s) also certify that the Deed conveying the property will contain a "hazardous waste clause."

12.   Seller(s) and Buyer(s) both agree to comply with the Federal Lead Disclosure Act and the _____ (State, if one) Real Estate Sales Disclosure Act Laws and to execute all required disclosure statements.

13.   Title to the aforementioned property will be transferred by General Warranty Deed, and title to said property will be good and marketable in the opinion of an attorney for the Buyer(s), based on a sixty-year (60) title examination to a good and sufficient General Warranty Deed. Any exceptions and reservations for oil, gas, and/or minerals in, on, and under the property existing in favor of another party in the chain of title will not be considered a defect in title or anything which would take away an otherwise good and marketable title to the real estate.

14.   Within _____ days of the execution of this Agreement, the Buyer(s), at their own expense, may choose to have inspections and/or certifications completed by licensed or otherwise qualified professional for said premises. Should the Buyer(s) choose to have a home inspection of the property, as defined in the _____ (State) Home Inspection Law, the home inspection must be completed by a full member in good standing of a national home inspection association, or by a person supervised by a full member of a national home inspection association, in accordance with the ethical standards and code of conduct or practice of that association. If the Buyer(s) is/are not satisfied with the condition of the premises as stated in any written report of such inspection, Buyer(s) will:

a.   Accept said property with the information stated in the given inspection report(s); or

b.   Terminate this Agreement within fifteen (15) days of the inspection by written notice to Seller(s), whereby any and all deposit monies paid toward the purchase price will be immediately returned to the Buyer(s) and this Agreement will be VOID; or

c.   Enter into a mutually acceptable written agreement with the Seller(s) providing for any repairs or improvements to the premises and/or any credit to

AGREEMENT FOR SALE OF COMMERCIAL REAL ESTATE

the Buyer(s) at settlement. Should the efforts to reach a mutually acceptable agreement fail, the Buyer(s) must then choose to accept said property or terminate this Agreement within the time as stated herein.

15. If Seller(s) is/are in default hereunder due to the failure of title or a fire/casualty that partially or completely destroys the premises, the Buyer(s), as their sole and exclusive remedies, may:

a. Terminate this Agreement by delivering written notices to the Seller(s) at or prior to the closing. In this case, any deposit and all interest earned thereon will belong to the Buyer(s) and Seller(s) shall have no further obligation or liability to the Buyer(s) and the Buyer(s) shall have no further rights hereunder.

Signed this _____ day of _____ (Month) _____ (Year).

WITNESSETH, both parties have executed this agreement at the day and year first above written.

_____

Seller Printed

_____

Seller Signature

_____

Buyer Printed

_____

Buyer Printed

APPENDIX E

In order for a Section 1031 exchange to be completely tax-free, you cannot receive any boot. Boot is a term you will not find in the Internal Revenue Code or Regulations. But it is commonly defined this way: Boot is the money or the fair market value of "other property" received by the taxpayer in a 1031 exchange. Money includes all forms of cash, including any liabilities the taxpayer takes on or passes to the other party. Other property refers to any property that is not like-kind, including personal property and non-qualified property. Any boot received is taxable (to the extent of gain realized on the exchange). Boot can be but is not always intentionally received and results from a variety of factors. That means it is important for you to understand what can result in boot if taxable income is to be avoided. The most common sources of boot include the following:

- Cash boot, which usually comes in the form of "net cash received." In other words, it is the difference between the cash received from the sale and the cash paid for the property. This can occur when a person is "trading down," as when the replacement property is less expensive than the property being sold.

- Debt reduction boot will occur if the debt on a replacement property is less than the debt on the sold property. This can also occur when a person is "trading down."

- Sale proceeds are those funds not related to closing costs. Some of the following may be categorized as sale proceeds:

  o Rent prorations

  o Utility escrow charges

  o Any other charges unrelated to the closing

AN EXPLANATION OF THE CONCEPT OF "BOOT"

- Excess borrowing refers to the instance in which a person borrows more money than is necessary. You must use all the cash being held by the intermediary or else boot will result.

- Loan acquisition are those costs related to the servicing of the replacement property and using the exchange funds at the closing. These costs include origination fees and other related fees.

- Non-like-kind property received in the exchange might include seller financing, promissory notes, and so on.

Here are the boot offset rules: Only the net boot received can be taxed. In determining how much net boot you received, some offsets are allowed and some are not, such as:

- Cash boot paid (i.e., the replacement property) will always offset the cash boot received (i.e., the relinquished property).

- Debt boot paid (i.e., the replacement property) will always offset the debt-reduction boot received (i.e., relinquished property).

- Cash boot paid will always offset the debt-reduction boot received.

- Debt boot paid will never offset the cash boot received.

- Exchange expenses (i.e., transaction and closing costs) paid (i.e., relinquished property and replacement property closings) will always offset the net cash boot received.

These rules are complicated and your tax advisor should be on top of them. However, here are some general rules regarding the boot:

- You should never trade down, which always results in boot received.

- Bring cash to the closing of the relinquished property to cover charges which are not transaction costs.

- Do not receive any not like-kind property in an exchange.

Do not over-finance the replacement property. You should only use the necessary amount to close on the replacement property.

AUTHOR BIOGRAPHY

Steven D. Fisher is an independent writer, illustrator, and instructional designer with over 25 years of experience in the fields of business writing and training and development. His specialties include the design and writing of books, certification tests, e-Books, manuals, seminars and workshops. In addition to practical "real world" experience, he holds an M.A. in Education of the Hearing Impaired and trained as a print and media Broadcast Specialist in the U.S. Army.

GLOSSARY

Abatement Sometimes referred to as free rent or early occupancy and could happen in addition to the primary term of the lease.

Above Building Standard Finishes and specialized designs that have been upgraded in order to accommodate a tenant's requirements.

Absorption Rate The speed and amount of time at which rentable space, in square feet, is filled.

Abstract or Title Search The process of reviewing all transactions that have been recorded publicly in order to determine whether any defects in the title exist that could interfere with a clear property ownership transfer.

Accelerated Cost Recovery System A calculation for taxes to provide more depreciation for the first few years of ownership.

Accelerated Depreciation A method of depreciation where the value of a property depreciates faster in the first few years after purchasing it.

Acceleration Clause A clause in a contract that gives the lender the right to demand immediate payment of the balance of the loan if the borrower defaults on the loan.

Acceptance The seller's written approval of a buyer's offer.

Ad Valorem A Latin phrase that translates as "according to value". Refers to a tax that is imposed on a property's value that is typically based on the local government's evaluation of the property.

Addendum Addition or update for an existing contract between parties.

Additional Principal Payment Additional money paid to the lender, apart from the scheduled loan payments, to pay more of the principal balance, shortening the length of the loan.

Adjustable-Rate Mortgage (ARM)

A home loan with an interest rate that is adjusted periodically in order to reflect changes in a specific financial resource.

Adjusted Funds From Operations (AFFO) The rate of REIT performance or ability to pay dividends that is used by many analysts who have concerns about the quality of earnings as measured by Funds From Operations (FFO).

Adjustment Date The date at which the interest rate is adjusted for an adjustable-rate mortgage (ARM).

Adjustment Period Amount of time between adjustments for an interest rate in an ARM.

Administrative Fee A percentage of the value of the assets under management, or a fixed annual dollar amount charged to manage an account.

Adviser A broker or investment banker who represents an owner in a transaction and is paid a retainer and/or a performance fee once a financing or sales transaction has closed.

Agency Closing A type of closing in which a lender uses a title company or other firm as an agent to finish a loan.

Agency Disclosure A requirement in most states that agents who act for both buyers or sellers must disclose who they are working for in the transaction.

Aggregation Risk The risk that is associated with warehousing mortgages during the process of pooling them for future security.

Agreement of Sale A legal document the buyer and seller must approve and sign that details the price and terms in the transaction.

Alternative Mortgage A home loan that does not match the standard terms of a fixed-rate mortgage.

Alternative or Specialty Investments Types of property not considered to be conventional real estate investments, such as self-storage facilities, mobile homes, timber, agriculture, or parking lots.

Amortization The usual process of paying a loan's interest and principal via scheduled monthly payments.

Amortization Schedule Chart or table that shows the percentage of each payment that will be applied toward principal and interest over the life of the mortgage and how the loan balance decreases until it reaches zero.

Amortization Tables The mathematical tables that are used to calculate what a borrower's monthly payment will be.

Amortization Term The number of months it will take to amortize the loan.

Anchor The business or individual who is serving as the primary draw to a commercial property.

Annual Mortgagor Statement A yearly statement to borrowers which details the remaining principal balance and amounts paid throughout the year for taxes and interest.

Annual Percentage Rate (APR) The interest rate that states the actual cost of borrowing money over the course of a year.

Annuity The regular payments of a fixed sum.

Appraisal The estimate of the value of a property on a particular date given by a professional appraiser, usually presented in a written document.

Appraisal Fee The fee charged by a professional appraiser for his estimate of the market value of a property.

Appraisal Report The written report presented by an appraiser regarding the value of a property.

Appraised Value Dollar amount a professional appraiser assigned to the value of a property in his report.

Appraiser A certified individual who is qualified by education, training, and experience to estimate the value of real and personal property.

Appreciation An increase in the home's or property's value.

Appreciation Return The amount gained when the value of the real estate assets increases during the current quarter.

ARM Index A number that is publicly published and used as the basis for interest rate adjustments on an ARM.

As-Is Condition A phrase in a purchase or lease contract in which the new tenant accepts the existing condition of the premises as well as any physical defects.

Assessed Value The value placed on a home that is determined by a tax assessor in order to calculate a tax base.

Assessment (1) The approximate value of a property. (2) A fee charged in addition to taxes in order to help pay for items such as water, sewer, street improvements, etc.

Assessor A public officer who estimates the value of a property for the purpose of taxation.

Asset A property or item of value owned by an individual or company.

Asset Management The various tasks and areas around managing real estate assets from the initial investment until the time it is sold.

Asset Turnover The rate of total revenues for the previous 12 months divided by the average total assets.

Assignee Name The individual or business to whom the lease, mortgage, or other contract has been re-assigned.

Assignment The transfer of rights and responsibilities from one party to another for paying a debt. The original party remains liable for the debt should the second party default.

Assignor The person who transfers the rights and interests of a property to another.

Assumable Mortgage A mortgage that is capable of being transferred to a different borrower.

Assumption Clause A contractual provision that enables the buyer to take responsibility for the mortgage loan from the seller.

Assumption Fee A fee charged to the buyer for processing new records when they are assuming an existing loan.

Average Occupancy Average rate of each of the previous 12 months that a property was occupied.

Average Total Assets Sum of total assets of a company for the previous five quarters divided by five.

Back Title Letter A letter that an attorney receives from a title insurance company before examining the title for insurance purposes.

Back-End Ratio The calculation lenders use to compare a borrower's gross monthly income to their total debt.

Balance Sheet A statement that lists an individual's assets, liabilities, and net worth.

Balloon Loan A type of mortgage in which the monthly payments are not large enough to repay the loan by the end of the term, and the final payment is one large payment of the remaining balance.

Balloon Payment Final payment due at end of balloon mortgages.

Balloon Risk The risk that a borrower may not be able to come up with the funds for the balloon payment at maturity.

Bankruptcy A legal proceeding where a debtor can obtain relief from payment of certain obligations through restructuring their finances.

Base Loan Amount The amount that forms the basis for the loan payments.

Base Principal Balance Original loan amount once adjustments for subsequent fundings and principal payments have been made without including accrued interest or other unpaid debts.

Base Rent A certain amount that is used as a minimum rent, providing for rent increases over the term of the lease agreement.

Base Year Sum of actual taxes and operating expenses during a given year, often that in which a lease begins.

Basis Point A term for 1/100 of one percentage point.

Before-Tax Income An individual's income before taxes have been deducted.

Below-Grade Any structure or part of a structure that is below the surface of the ground that surrounds it.

Bill of Sale A written legal document that transfers the ownership of personal property to another party.

Binder (1) A report describing the conditions of a property's title. (2) An early agreement between seller and buyer.

Biweekly Mortgage A mortgage repayment plan that requires payments every two weeks to help repay the loan over a shorter amount of time.

Blanket Mortgage A rare type of mortgage that covers more than one of the borrower's properties.

Book Value Value of a property based on its purchase amount plus upgrades or other additions with depreciation subtracted.

Break-Even Point The point at which a landlord's income from rent matches expenses and debt.

Bridge Loan Short-term loan for individuals or companies still seeking more permanent financing.

Broker A person who serves as a go-between for a buyer and seller. **243**

Brokerage The process of bringing two or more parties together in exchange for a fee, commission, or other compensation.

Buildable Acres The portion of land that can be built on after allowances for roads, setbacks, anticipated open spaces, and unsuitable areas have been made.

Building Code Laws set forth by local governments regarding end use of a given piece of property. These law codes may dictate the design, materials used, and/or types of improvements that will be allowed.

Building Standard Plus Allowance A detailed list provided by the landlord stating the standard building materials and costs necessary to make the premises inhabitable.

Build-Out Improvements to a property's space that have been implemented according to the tenant's specifications.

Build-to-Suit A way of leasing property, usually for commercial purposes, in which the developer or landlord builds to a tenant's specifications.

Buydown A term that usually refers to a fixed-rate mortgage for which additional payments can be applied to the interest rate for a temporary period, lowering payments for a period of one to three years.

Buydown Mortgage A style of home loan in which the lender receives a higher payment in order to convince them to reduce the interest rate during the initial years of the mortgage.

Call Date The periodic or continuous right a lender has to call for payment of the total remaining balance prior to the date of maturity.

Call Option A clause in a loan agreement that allows a lender to demand repayment of the entire principal balance at any time.

Cap A limit on how much the monthly payment or interest rate is allowed to increase in an adjustable-rate mortgage.

Capital Appreciation Change in a property's or portfolio's market value after it has been adjusted for capital improvements and partial sales.

Capital Gain The amount of excess when the net proceeds from the sale of an asset are higher than its book value.

Capital Improvements Expenses

that prolong the life of a property or add new improvements to it.

Capital Markets Public and private markets where individuals or businesses can raise or borrow capital.

Capitalization The mathematical process that investors use to derive the value of a property using the rate of return on investments.

Capitalization Rate Percentage of return as it is estimated from the net income of a property.

Carryback Financing A type of funding in which a seller agrees to hold back a note for a specified portion of the sales price.

Cash Flow Amount of income an investor receives on a rental property after operating expenses and loan payments have been deducted.

Cash-on-Cash Yield The percentage of a property's net cash flow and the average amount of invested capital during the specified operating year.

Cash-Out Refinance Act of refinancing a mortgage for an amount higher than the original amount for the purpose of using the leftover cash for personal use.

Certificate of Eligibility Type of document that the Department of Veterans Affairs issues to verify eligibility of a veteran for a VA loan.

Certificate of Occupancy (CO) A written document issued by a local government or building agency that states that a home or other building is inhabitable after meeting all building codes.

Certificate of Reasonable Value (CRV) An appraisal presented by the Department of Veterans Affairs that shows the current market value of a property.

Certificate of Veteran Status A document veterans or reservists receive if they have served 90 days of continuous active duty (including training time).

Chain of Title The official record of all transfers of ownership over the history of a piece of property.

Chapter 11 The part of the federal bankruptcy code that deals with reorganizations of businesses.

Chapter 7 The part of the federal bankruptcy code that deals with liquidations of businesses.

Circulation Factor The interior space that is required for internal office circulation and is not included in the net square footage.

Class A A property rating that is usually assigned to those that will generate the maximum rent per square foot, due to superior quality and/or location.

Class B A good property that most potential tenants would find desirable but lacks certain attributes that would bring in the top dollar.

Class C A building that is physically acceptable but offers few amenities, thereby becoming cost-effective space for tenants who are seeking a particular image.

Clear Title A property title that is free of liens, defects, or other legal encumbrances.

Clear-Span Facility A type of building, usually a warehouse or parking garage, consisting of vertical columns on the outer edges of the structure and clear spaces between the columns.

Closed-End Fund A mixed fund with a planned range of investor capital and a limited life.

Closing Final act of procuring a loan and title in which documents are signed between the buyer and seller and/or their respective representation and all money concerned in the contract changes hands.

Closing Costs The expenses that are related to the sale of real estate including loan, title, and appraisal fees and are beyond the price of the property itself.

Cloud on Title Certain conditions uncovered in a title search that present a negative impact to the title for the property.

Commercial Mortgage-Backed Securities (CMBS) A type of securities that is backed by loans on commercial real estate.

Collateralized Mortgage Obligation (CMO) Debt that is fully based on a pool of mortgages.

Co-Borrower Another individual who is jointly responsible for the loan and is on the title to the property.

Co-Investment Program A separate account for an insurance company or investment partnership in which two or more pension funds may co-invest their capital in an individual property or a portfolio of properties.

Co-Investment Condition that occurs when two or more pension funds or groups of funds are sharing ownership of an investment.

Collateral The property for which a borrower has obtained a loan, thereby assuming the risk of losing the property if the loan is not repaid according to the terms of the loan agreement.

Commercial Mortgage A loan used to purchase a piece of commercial property or building.

Commercial Mortgage Broker A broker specialized in commercial mortgage applications.

Commercial Mortgage Lender A lender specialized in funding commercial mortgage loans.

Commission A compensation to salespeople that is paid out of the total amount of the purchase transaction.

Commitment The agreement of a lender to make a loan with given terms for a specific period.

Commitment Fee The fee a lender charges for the guarantee of specified loan terms, to be honored at some point in the future.

Common Area Assessments Sometimes called Homeowners' Association Fees. Charges paid to the homeowners' association by the individual unit owners, in a condominium or planned unit development (PUD), that are usually used to maintain the property and common areas.

Common Area Maintenance Additional charges tenants must pay in addition to the base rent to pay for the maintenance of common areas.

Common Areas Portions of a building, land, and amenities, owned or managed by a planned unit development (PUD) or condominium's HOA, that are used by all of the unit owners who share in the common expense of operation and maintenance.

Community Property Property that is acquired by a married couple during the course of their marriage and is considered in many states to be owned jointly, unless certain circumstances are in play.

Comparable Sales Also called Comps or Comparables. The recent selling prices of similar properties in the area that are used to help determine the market value of a property.

Compound Interest The amount of interest paid on the principal balance of a mortgage in addition to accrued interest.

Condemnation A government agency's act of taking private property, without the owner's consent, for public use through the power of eminent domain.

Conditional Commitment A lender's agreement to make a loan providing the borrower meets certain conditions.

Conditional Sale Contract to sell a property that states the seller will retain the title until all contractual conditions have been fulfilled.

Condominium A type of ownership in which all of the unit owners own the property, common areas, and buildings jointly, and have sole ownership in the unit to which they hold the title.

Condominium Conversion Changing an existing rental property's ownership to the condominium form of ownership.

Conduit A strategic alliance between lenders and unaffiliated organizations that acts as a source of funding by regularly purchasing loans, usually with a goal of pooling and securitizing them.

Conforming Loan A type of mortgage that meets the conditions to be purchased by Fannie Mae or Freddie Mac.

Construction Documents The drawings and specifications an architect and/or engineer provides to describe construction requirements for a project.

Construction Loan A short-term loan to finance the cost of construction, usually dispensed in stages throughout the construction project.

Construction Management Process of ensuring the stages of the construction project are completed in a timely and seamless manner.

Construction-to-Permanent Loan A construction loan that can be converted to a longer-term traditional mortgage after construction is complete.

Contiguous Space Refers to several suites or spaces on a floor (or connected floors) in a given building that can be combined and rented to a single tenant.

Contingency A specific condition that must be met before either party in a contract can be legally bound.

Contract An agreement, either verbal or written, to perform or not to perform a certain thing.

Contract Rent Also known as Face Rent. The dollar amount of the rental obligation specified in a lease.

Conventional Loan A long-term loan from a non-governmental lender that a borrower obtains for the purchase of a home.

Convertible Adjustable-Rate Mortgage Mortgage that begins as a traditional ARM but contains a provision to enable the borrower to change to a fixed-rate mortgage during a certain period of time.

Convertible Debt The point in a mortgage at which the lender has the option to convert to a partially or fully owned property within a certain period of time.

Convertible Preferred Stock Preferred stock that can be converted to common stock under certain conditions that have been specified by the issuer.

Conveyance The act of transferring a property title between parties by deed.

Cooperative Also called a Co-op. A type of ownership by multiple residents of a multi-unit housing complex in which they all own shares in the cooperative corporation that owns the property, thereby having the right to occupy a particular apartment or unit.

Cooperative Mortgage Any loan that is related to a cooperative residential project.

Core Properties The main types of property, specifically office, retail, industrial, and multi-family.

Co-Signer A second individual or party who also signs a promissory note or loan agreement, thereby taking responsibility for the debt in the event that the primary borrower cannot pay.

Cost-Approach Improvement Value The current expenses for constructing a copy or replacement for an existing structure, but subtracting an estimate of the accrued depreciation.

Cost-Approach Land Value The estimated value of the basic interest in the land, as if it were available for development to its highest and best use.

Cost-of-Sale Percentage Estimate of the expenses of selling an investment that represents brokerage commissions, closing costs, fees, and other necessary sales costs.

Covenant A written agreement, included in deeds or other legal documents, that defines the requirements for certain acts or use of a property.

Credit Enhancement The necessary credit support, in addition to mortgage collateral, in order to achieve the desired credit rating on mortgage-backed securities.

Credit History An individual's

record which details his current and past financial obligations and performance.

Credit Rating The degree of creditworthiness a person is assigned based on his credit history and current financial status.

Credit Report A record detailing an individual's credit, employment, and residence history used to determine the individual's creditworthiness.

Credit Repository A company that records and updates credit applicants' financial and credit information from various sources.

Credit Score Sometimes called a Credit Risk Score. The number contained in a consumer's credit report that represents a statistical summary of the information.

Creditor A party to whom other parties owe money.

Cross-Collateralization A group of mortgages or properties that jointly secures one debt obligation.

Cross-Defaulting A provision that allows a trustee or lender to require full payment on all loans in a group, if any single loan in the group is in default.

250 **Cumulative Discount Rate** A

percentage of the current value of base rent with all landlord lease concessions taken into account.

Current Occupancy The current percentage of units in a building or property that is leased.

Current Yield The annual rate of return on an investment, expressed as a percentage.

Deal Structure The type of agreement in financing an acquisition. The deal can be un-leveraged, leveraged, traditional debt, participating debt, participating/convertible debt, or joint ventures.

Debt Any amount one party owes to another party.

Debt Service Coverage Ratio (DSCR) A property's yearly net operating income divided by the yearly cost of debt service.

Debt Service The amount of money that is necessary to meet all interest and principal payments during a specific period.

Debt-to-Income Ratio The percentage of a borrower's monthly payment on long-term debts divided by his gross monthly income.

Dedicate To change a private

property to public ownership for a particular public use.

Deed Legal document that conveys property ownership to the buyer.

Deed in Lieu of Foreclosure A situation in which a deed is given to a lender in order to satisfy a mortgage debt and to avoid the foreclosure process.

Deed of Trust A provision that allows a lender to foreclose on a property in the event that the borrower defaults on the loan.

Default The state that occurs when a borrow fails to fulfill a duty or take care of an obligation, such as making monthly mortgage payments.

Deferred Maintenance Account A type of account that a borrower must fund to provide for maintenance of a property.

Deficiency Judgment The legal assignment of personal liability to a borrower for the unpaid balance of a mortgage, after foreclosing on the property has failed to yield the full amount of the debt.

Delinquency A state that occurs when the borrower fails to make mortgage payments on time, eventually resulting in foreclosure, if severe enough.

Delinquent Mortgage A mortgage in which the borrower is behind on payments.

Demising Wall Physical partition between spaces of two tenants or from the building's common areas.

Deposit Also referred to as Earnest Money. The funds that the buyer provides when offering to purchase property.

Depreciation A decline in the value of property or an asset, often used as a tax-deductible item.

Derivative Securities A type of securities that has been created from other financial instruments.

Disclosure A written statement, presented to a potential buyer, that lists information relevant to a piece of property, whether positive or negative.

Discount Points Fees that a lender charges in order to provide a lower interest rate.

Discount Rate A figure used to translate present value from future payments or receipts.

Distraint The act of seizing a tenant's personal property when the tenant is in default, based on the right the landlord has in satisfying the debt.

Diversification Act of spreading individual investments out to insulate a portfolio against the risk of reduced yield or capital loss.

Document Needs List The list of documents a lender requires from a potential borrower who is submitting a loan application.

Documentation Preparation Fee A fee that lenders, brokers, and/or settlement agents charge for the preparation of the necessary closing documents.

Dollar Stop An agreed amount of taxes and operating expenses each tenant must pay out on a prorated basis.

Down Payment The variance between the purchase price and the portion that the mortgage lender financed.

DOWNREIT A structure of organization that makes it possible for REITs to purchase properties using partnership units.

Draw A payment from the construction loan proceeds made to contractors, subcontractors, home builders, or suppliers.

Due Diligence The activities of a prospective purchaser or mortgager of real property for the purpose of confirming that the property is as

represented by the seller and is not subject to environmental or other problems.

Due on Sale Clause The standard mortgage language that states the loan must still be repaid if the property is resold.

Earthquake Insurance Type of insurance policy that provides coverage against earthquake damage.

Easement The right given to a non-ownership party to use a certain part of the property for specified purposes, such as servicing power lines or cable lines.

Economic Feasibility Viability of a building or project in terms of costs and revenue where the degree of viability is established by extra revenue.

Economic Rent The market rental value of a property at a particular point in time.

Effective Age An estimate of the physical condition of a building presented by an appraiser.

Effective Date The date on which the sale of securities can commence once a registration statement becomes effective.

Effective Gross Income (EGI) Total property income that rents and other sources generate after subtracting a vacancy factor estimated to be appropriate for the property.

Effective Gross Rent (EGR) Net rent that is generated after adjusting for tenant improvements and other capital costs, lease commissions, and other sales expenses.

Effective Rent Actual rental rate the landlord achieves after deducting the concession value from the base rental rate a tenant pays.

Eminent Domain The power of the government to pay the fair market value for a property, appropriating it for public use.

Encroachment Any improvement or upgrade that illegally intrudes onto another party's property.

Encumbrance Any right or interest in a property that interferes with using it or transferring ownership.

End Loan The result of converting to permanent financing from a construction loan.

Entitlement Benefit of a VA home loan. Often referred to as Eligibility.

Environmental Impact Statement Legally required documents that must accompany major project proposals where an impact on the surrounding environment is likely.

Equal Credit Opportunity Act (ECOA) A federal law that requires a lender or other creditor to make credit available for applicants regardless of sex, marital status, race, religion, or age.

Equifax One of the three primary credit-reporting bureaus.

Equity Value of a property after existing liabilities are deducted.

Employee Retirement Income Security Act (ERISA) A legislation that controls the investment activities, mainly of corporate and union pension plans.

Errors and Omissions Insurance Type of policy that insures against the mistakes of a builder or architect.

Escalation Clause The clause in a lease that provides for the rent to be increased to account for increases in the expenses the landlord must pay.

Escrow A valuable item, money, or documents deposited with a third party for delivery upon the fulfillment of a condition.

Escrow Account Also: Impound Account. Account established by a mortgage lender or servicing company for the purpose of holding funds for the payment of items, such as homeowner's insurance and property taxes.

Escrow Agent A neutral third party who makes sure that all conditions of a real estate transaction have been met before any funds are transferred or property is recorded.

Escrow Agreement A written agreement between an escrow agent and the contractual parties that defines the basic obligations of each party, the money (or other valuables) to be deposited in escrow, and how the escrow agent is to dispose of the money on deposit.

Escrow Closing The event in which all conditions of a real estate transaction have been met, and the property title is transferred to the buyer.

Escrow Company A neutral company that serves as a third party to ensure that all conditions of a real estate transaction are met.

Escrow Disbursements Dispensing of escrow funds for payment of real estate taxes, hazard insurance, mortgage insurance, and other property expenses as they are due.

Escrow Payment Funds that are withdrawn by a mortgage servicer from a borrower's escrow account to pay property taxes and insurance.

Estate Total assets, including

property, of an individual after he has died.

Estimated Closing Costs An estimation of the expenses relating to the sale of real estate.

Estimated Hazard Insurance An estimation of hazard insurance, or homeowner's insurance, that will cover physical risks.

Estimated Property Taxes Estimation of property taxes that must be paid on the property, according to state/ county tax rates.

Estoppel Certificate A signed statement that certifies that certain factual statements are correct as of the date of the statement and can be relied upon by a third party, such as a prospective lender or purchaser.

Eviction The legal removal of an occupant from a piece of property.

Examination of Title A title company's inspection and report of public records and other documents for the purpose of determining the chain of ownership of a property.

Executed Contract An agreement in which all parties involved have fulfilled their duties.

Executor Individual who is named in a will to administer an estate. Executrix is the feminine form.

Exit Strategy An approach investors may use when they wish to liquidate all or part of their investment.

Experian One of the three primary credit-reporting bureaus.

Facility Space The floor area in a hospitality property that is dedicated to activities, such as restaurants, health clubs, and gift shops, that interactively service multiple people and is not directly related to room occupancy.

Funds Available for Distribution (FAD) The income from operations, with cash expenditures subtracted, that may be used for leasing commissions and tenant improvement costs.

FAD Multiple The price per share of a REIT divided by its funds available for distribution.

Fair Credit Reporting Act (FCRA) The federal legislation that governs the processes credit reporting agencies must follow.

Fair Housing Act The federal legislation that prohibits the refusal to rent or sell to anyone based on race, color, religion, sex, family status, or disability.

Fair Market Value The highest price that a buyer would be willing to pay, and the lowest a seller would be willing to accept.

Fannie Mae's Community Home Buyer's Program A community lending model based on borrower income in which mortgage insurers and Fannie Mae offer flexible underwriting guidelines in order to increase the buying power for a low- or moderate-income family and to decrease the total amount of cash needed to purchase a home.

Farmer's Home Administration (FMHA) An agency within the U.S. Department of Agriculture that provides credit to farmers and other rural residents.

Federal Home Loan Mortgage Corporation (FHLMC) Also known as Freddie Mac. The company that buys mortgages from lending institutions, combines them with other loans, and sells shares to investors.

Federal Housing Administration (FHA) A government agency that provides low-rate mortgages to buyers who are able to make a down payment as low as 3 percent.

Federal National Mortgage Association (FNMA) Also known as Fannie Mae. A congressionally chartered, shareholder-owned company that is the nation's largest supplier of home mortgage funds. The company buys mortgages from lenders and resells them as securities on the secondary mortgage market.

Fee Simple The highest possible interest a person can have in a piece of real estate.

Fee Simple Estate Unconditional, unlimited inheritance estate in which the owner may dispose of or use the property as desired.

Fee Simple Interest State of owning all rights in a real estate parcel.

Funds From Operations (FFO) A ratio that is meant to highlight the amount of cash a company's real estate portfolio generates relative to its total operating cash flow.

FHA Loans Mortgages that the Federal Housing Administration (FHA) insures.

FHA Mortgage Insurance A type of insurance that requires a fee to be paid at closing in order to insure the loan with the Federal Housing Administration (FHA).

Fiduciary Any individual who holds authority over a plan's asset management, administration or disposition, or renders paid investment advice regarding a plan's assets.

Finance Charge The amount of interest to be paid on a loan or credit card balance.

Firm Commitment A written agreement a lender makes to loan money for the purchase of property.

First Mortgage The main mortgage on a property.

First Refusal Right/ Right of First Refusal A lease clause that gives a tenant the first opportunity to buy a property or to lease additional space in a property at the same price and terms as those contained in an offer from a third party that the owner has expressed a willingness to accept.

Fixed Costs Expenses that remain the same despite the level of sales or production.

Fixed Rate An interest rate that does not change over the life of the loan.

Fixed Time The particular weeks of a year that the owner of a timeshare arrangement can access his or her accommodations.

Fixed-Rate Mortgage A loan with an unchanging interest rate over the life of the loan.

Flat Fee An amount of money that an adviser or manager receives for managing a portfolio of real estate assets.

Flex Space A building that provides a flexible configuration of office or showroom space combined with manufacturing, laboratory, warehouse, distribution, etc.

Flood Certification The process of analyzing whether a property is located in a known flood zone.

Flood Insurance A policy that is required in designated flood zones to protect against loss due to flood damage.

Floor Area Ratio (FAR) A measurement of a building's gross square footage compared to the square footage of the land on which it is located.

For Sale By Owner (FSBO) A method of selling property in which the property owner serves as the selling agent and directly handles the sales process with the buyer or buyer's agent.

Foreclosure The legal process in which a lender takes over ownership of a property once the borrower is in default in a mortgage arrangement.

Forward Commitments Contractual agreements to perform certain financing duties according to any stated conditions.

Four Quadrants of the Real Estate Capital Markets The four market types that consist of Private Equity, Public Equity, Private Debt, and Public Debt.

Front-End Ratio Measurement a lender uses to compare a borrower's monthly housing expense to gross monthly income.

Full Recourse A loan on which the responsibility of a loan is transferred to an endorser or guarantor in the event of default by the borrower.

Fully Amortized ARM An ARM with a monthly payment that is sufficient to amortize the remaining balance at the current interest accrual rate over the amortization term.

Future Proposed Space The space in a commercial development that has been proposed but is not yet under construction, or the future phases of a multi-phase project that has not yet been built.

General Contractor The main person or business that contracts for the construction of an entire building or project, rather than individual duties.

General Partner The member in a

partnership who holds the authority to bind the partnership and shares in its profits and losses.

Going-In Capitalization Rate The rate that is computed by dividing the expected net operating income for the first year by the value of the property.

Good Faith Estimate A lender's or broker's estimate that shows all costs associated with obtaining a home loan including loan processing, title, and inspection fees.

Government Loan A mortgage that is insured or guaranteed by the FHA, the Department of Veterans Affairs (VA), or the Rural Housing Service (RHS).

Government National Mortgage Association (GNMA) Also known as Ginnie Mae. A government-owned corporation under the U.S. Department of Housing and Urban Development (HUD) that performs the same role as Fannie Mae and Freddie Mac in providing funds to lenders for making home loans, but only purchases loans that are backed by the federal government.

Grace Period A defined time period in which a borrower may make a loan payment after its due date without incurring a penalty.

Graduated Lease A lease, usually long-term, in which rent payments vary in accordance with future contingencies.

Graduated Payment Mortgage A mortgage that requires low payments during the first years of the loan, but eventually requires larger monthly payments over the term of the loan that become fixed later in the term.

Grant To give or transfer an interest in a property by deed or other documented method.

Grantee The party to whom an interest in a property is given.

Grantor Party who is transferring an interest in a property.

Gross Building Area The sum of areas at all floor levels, including the basement, mezzanine, and penthouses included in the principal outside faces of the exterior walls without allowing for architectural setbacks or projections.

Gross Income The total income of a household before taxes or expenses have been subtracted.

Gross Investment in Real Estate (Historic Cost) The total amount of equity and debt that is invested in a piece of real estate minus proceeds from sales or partial sales.

Gross Leasable Area Amount of floor space designed for tenants' occupancy and exclusive use.

Gross Lease A rental arrangement in which the tenant pays a flat sum for rent, and the landlord must pay all building expenses out of that amount.

Gross Real Estate Asset Value The total market value of the real estate investments under management in a fund or individual accounts, usually including the total value of all equity positions, debt positions, and joint venture ownership positions.

Gross Real Estate Investment Value The market value of real estate investments that are held in a portfolio without including debt.

Gross Returns The investment returns generated from operating a property without adjusting for adviser or manager fees.

Ground Lease Land being leased to an individual that has absolutely no residential dwelling on the property; or if it does, the ground (or land) is the only portion of the property being leased.

Ground Rent A long-term lease in which rent is paid to the land owner, normally to build something on that land.

Growing-Equity Mortgage A fixed-rate mortgage in which payments increase over a specified amount of time with the extra funds being applied to the principal.

Guarantor The part who makes a guaranty.

Guaranty An agreement in which the guarantor promises to satisfy the debt or obligations of another, if and when the debtor fails to do so.

Hard Cost The expenses attributed to actually constructing property improvements.

Hazard Insurance Also known as Homeowner's Insurance or Fire Insurance. A policy that provides coverage for damage from forces such as fire and wind.

Highest and Best Use The most reasonable, expected, legal use of a piece of vacant land or improved property that is physically possible, supported appropriately, financially feasible, and that results in the highest value.

High-Rise In a suburban district, any building taller than six stories.

In a business district, any building taller than 25 stories.

Holding Period Expected length of time, from purchase to sale, that an investor will own a property.

Hold-Over Tenant A tenant who retains possession of the leased premises after the lease has expired.

Home Equity Conversion Mortgage (HECM) Also referred to as a Reverse Annuity Mortgage. A type of mortgage in which the lender makes payments to the owner, thereby enabling older homeowners to convert equity in their homes into cash in the form of monthly payments.

Home Equity Line An open-ended amount of credit based on the equity a homeowner has accumulated.

Home Equity Loan A type of loan that allows owners to borrow against the equity in their homes up to a limited amount.

Home Inspection A pre-purchase examination of the condition a home is in by a certified inspector.

Home Inspector A certified professional who determines the structural soundness and operating systems of a property.

Homeowners' Association (HOA) A group that governs a community, condominium building, or neighborhood and enforces the covenants, conditions, and restrictions set by the developer.

Homeowners' Association Dues The monthly payments that are paid to the homeowners' association for maintenance and communal expenses.

Homeowner's Insurance A policy that includes coverage for all damages that may affect the value of a house as defined in the terms of the insurance policy.

Homeowner's Warranty A type of policy home buyers often purchase to cover repairs, such as heating or air-conditioning, should they stop working within the coverage period.

Housing Expense Ratio Percentage of gross income that is devoted to housing costs each month.

HUD (Housing and Urban Development) A federal agency that oversees a variety of housing and community development programs, including the FHA.

HUD Median Income The average income for families in a particular area, which is estimated by HUD.

HUD-1 Settlement Statement
Also known as Closing Statement
or Settlement Sheet. An itemized
listing of the funds paid at closing.

**HUD-1 Uniform Settlement
Statement** A closing statement for
the buyer and seller that describes
all closing costs for a real estate
transaction or refinancing.

HVAC Heating, ventilating, and
air-conditioning.

Hybrid Debt A position in a
mortgage that has equity-like
features of participation in both
cash flow and the appreciation of
the property at the point of sale or
refinance.

Implied Cap Rate The net
operating income divided by
the sum of a REIT's equity
market capitalization and its total
outstanding debt.

Impounds Part of the monthly
mortgage payment that is reserved
in an account in order to pay for
hazard insurance, property taxes,
and private mortgage insurance.

Improvements The upgrades or
changes made to a building to
improve its value or usefulness.

Incentive Fee A structure in which
the fee amount charged is based on

the performance of the real estate
assets under management.

Income Capitalization Value
Figure derived for an income-
producing property by converting
its expected benefits into property
value.

Income Property A particular
property used to generate income
but not occupied by the owner.

Income Return The percentage of
the total return generated by the
income from property, fund, or
account operations.

Indirect Costs Expenses of
development other than the costs
of direct material and labor that are
related directly to the construction
of improvements.

Inflation The rate at which
consumer prices increase each year.

Initial Interest Rate The original
interest rate on an ARM which
is sometimes subject to a variety
of adjustments throughout the
mortgage.

Initial Rate Cap Limit specified
by some ARMs as the maximum
amount the interest rate may
increase when the initial interest
rate expires.

Initial Rate Duration Date

specified by most ARMs at which the initial rate expires.

Inspection Fee The fee that a licensed property inspector charges for determining the current physical condition of the property.

Inspection Report Written report of the property's condition presented by a licensed inspection professional.

Institutional-Grade Property A variety of types of real estate properties usually owned or financed by tax-exempt institutional investors.

Insured Mortgage A mortgage that is guaranteed by the FHA or by private mortgage insurance (PMI).

Interest Accrual Rate The rate at which a mortgage accrues interest.

Interest-Only Loan A mortgage for which the borrower pays only the interest that accrues on the loan balance each month.

Interest Rate The percentage that is charged for a loan.

Interest Rate Cap The highest interest rate charge allowed on the monthly payment of an ARM during an adjustment period.

Interest The price that is paid for the use of capital.

Internal Rate of Return (IRR) The calculation of a discounted cash flow analysis that is used to determine the potential total return of a real estate asset during a particular holding period.

Investment Committee The governing body that is charged with overseeing corporate pension investments and developing investment policies for board approval.

Investment Manager An individual or company that assumes authority over a specified amount of real estate capital, invests that capital in assets using a separate account, and provides asset management.

Investment Policy A document that formalizes an institution's goals, objectives, and guidelines for asset management, investment advisory contracting, fees, and utilization of consultants and other outside professionals.

Investment Property A piece of real estate that generates some form of income.

Investment Strategy The methods used by a manager in structuring a portfolio and selecting the real estate assets for a fund or an account.

Investment Structures Approaches to investing that include un-leveraged acquisitions, leveraged acquisitions, traditional debt, participating debt, convertible debt, triple-net leases, and joint ventures.

Investment-Grade CMBS Commercial mortgage-backed securities that have ratings of AAA, AA, A, or BBB.

Investor Status The position an investor is in, either taxable or tax-exempt.

Joint Liability The condition in which responsibility rests with two or more people for fulfilling the terms of a home loan or other financial debt.

Joint Tenancy Form of ownership in which two or more people have equal shares in a piece of property, and rights pass to the surviving owner(s) in the event of death.

Joint Venture An investment business formed by more than one party for the purpose of acquiring or developing and managing property and/or other assets.

Judicial Foreclosure The usual foreclosure proceeding some states use, which is handled in a civil lawsuit.

Jumbo Loan A type of mortgage that exceeds the required limits set by Fannie Mae and Freddie Mac each year.

Junior Mortgage A loan that is a lower priority behind the primary loan.

Late Charge Fee imposed by a lender when the borrower has not made a payment when it was due.

Late Payment Payment made to the lender after the due date has passed.

Lease A contract between a property owner and tenant that defines payments and conditions under which the tenant may occupy the real estate for a given period of time.

Lease Commencement Date The date at which the terms of the lease are implemented.

Lease Expiration Exposure Schedule A chart of the total square footage of all current leases that expire in each of the next five years, without taking renewal options into account.

Lease Option A financing option that provides for homebuyers to lease a home with an option to buy, with part of the rental payments being applied toward the down payment.

Leasehold Limited right to inhabit a piece of real estate held by a tenant.

Leasehold State A way of holding a property title in which the mortgagor does not actually own the property but has a long-term lease on it.

Leasehold Interest The right to hold or use property for a specific period of time at a given price without transferring ownership.

Lease-Purchase A contract that defines the closing date and solutions for the seller in the event that the buyer defaults.

Legal Blemish A negative count against a piece of property such as a zoning violation or fraudulent title claim.

Legal Description A way of describing and locating a piece of real estate that is recognized by law.

Legal Owner The party who holds the title to the property, although the title may carry no actual rights to the property other than as a lien.

Lender A bank or other financial institution that offers home loans.

Leverage Process of increasing the return on an investment by borrowing some of the funds at an interest rate less than the return on the project.

Liabilities Borrower's debts and financial obligations, whether long- or short-term.

Liability Insurance A type of policy that protects owners against negligence, personal injury, or property damage claims.

London InterBank Offered Rate (LIBOR) The interest rate offered on Eurodollar deposits traded between banks and used to determine changes in interest rate for ARMs.

Lien A claim put by one party on the property of another as collateral for money owed.

Lien Waiver A waiver of a mechanic's lien rights that is sometimes required before the general contractor can receive money under the payment provisions of a construction loan and contract.

Lifecycle The stages of development for a property: pre-development, development, leasing, operating, and rehabilitation.

Like-Kind Property A term that refers to real estate that is held for productive use in a trade or business or for investment.

Limited Partnership A type of partnership in which some partners manage the business and are personally liable for partnership debts, but some partners contribute capital and share in profits without the responsibility of management.

Line of Credit Amount of credit granted by a financial institution up to a specified amount for a certain period of time to a borrower.

Liquid Asset A type of asset that can be easily converted into cash.

Liquidity The ease with which an individual's or company's assets can be converted to cash without losing their value.

Loan Amount of money borrowed and usually repaid with interest.

Loan Application A document that presents a borrower's income, debt, and other obligations to determine credit worthiness, as well as some basic information on the target property.

Loan Application Fee Fee lenders charge to cover expenses relating to reviewing a loan application.

Loan Commitment An agreement by a lender or other financial institution to make or ensure a loan for the specified amount and terms.

Loan Origination The process of obtaining and arranging new loans.

Loan Origination Fee A fee lenders charge to cover costs related to arranging the loan.

Loan Servicing Process a lending institution goes through for all loans it manages & involves processing payments, sending statements, managing the escrow/impound account, providing collection services on delinquent loans, ensuring that insurance and property taxes are made on the property, handling pay-offs and assumptions, as well as various other services.

Loan Term Time, usually expressed in years, that a lender sets in which a buyer must pay a mortgage.

Loan-to-Value (LTV) The ratio of the amount of the loan compared to the appraised value or sales price.

Lock-In A commitment from a lender to a borrower to guarantee a given interest rate for a limited amount of time.

Lock-In Period The period of

time during which the borrower is guaranteed a specified interest rate.

Lockout The period of time during which a loan may not be paid off early.

Long-Term Lease A rental agreement that will last at least three years from initial signing to the date of expiration or renewal.

Lot One of several contiguous parcels of a larger piece of land.

Low-Documentation Loan A mortgage that requires only a basic verification of income and assets.

Low-Rise A building that involves fewer than four stories above the ground level.

Lump-Sum Contract A type of construction contract that requires the general contractor to complete a building project for a fixed cost that is usually established beforehand by competitive bidding.

Maintenance Fee The charge to homeowners' association members each month for the repair and maintenance of common areas.

Margin A percentage that is added to the index and fixed for the mortgage term.

Market Capitalization A

measurement of a company's value that is calculated by multiplying the current share price by the current number of shares outstanding.

Market Rental Rates The rental income that a landlord could most likely ask for a property in the open market, indicated by the current rents for comparable spaces.

Market Study A forecast of the demand for a certain type of real estate project in the future that includes an estimate of the square footage that could be absorbed and the rents that could be charged.

Market Value The price a property would sell for at a particular point in time in a competitive market.

Marketable Title Title free of encumbrances and can be marketed immediately to a willing purchaser.

Master Lease The primary lease that controls other subsequent leases and may cover more property than all subsequent leases combined.

Maturity Date The date at which the total principal balance of a loan is due.

Metes and Bounds The surveyed boundary lines of a piece of land described by listing the compass directions (bounds) and distances (metes) of the boundaries.

Mezzanine Financing A financing position somewhere between equity and debt, meaning that there are higher-priority debts above and equity below.

Mid-Rise A building which shows 4 to 8 stories above ground level. In a business district, buildings up to 25 stories may also be included.

Modern Portfolio Theory (MPT) Approach of quantifying risk and return in an asset portfolio which emphasizes the portfolio rather than the individual assets and how the assets perform in relation to each other.

Modification Adjustment in the terms of a loan agreement.

Modified Annual Percentage Rate (APR) An index of the cost of a loan based on the standard APR but adjusted for the amount of time the borrower expects to hold the loan.

Mortgage An amount of money that is borrowed to purchase a property using that property as collateral.

Mortgage Acceleration Clause A provision enabling a lender to require that the rest of the loan

balance is paid in a lump sum under certain circumstances.

Mortgage Banker A financial institution that provides home loans using its own resources, often selling them to investors such as insurance companies or Fannie Mae.

Mortgage Broker An individual who matches prospective borrowers with lenders that the broker is approved to deal with.

Mortgage Constant A figure comparing an amortizing mortgage payment to the outstanding mortgage balance.

Mortgage Insurance (MI) A policy, required by lenders on some loans, that covers the lender against certain losses that are incurred as a result of a default on a home loan.

Mortgage Insurance Premium (MIP) The amount charged for mortgage insurance, either to a government agency or to a private MI company.

Mortgage Interest Deduction The tax write-off that the IRS allows most homeowners to deduct for annual interest payments made on real estate loans.

Mortgage Life and Disability

Insurance A type of term life insurance borrowers often purchase to cover debt that is left when the borrower dies or becomes too disabled to make the mortgage payments.

Mortgagee The financial institution that lends money to the borrower.

Mortgagor The person who requests to borrow money to purchase a property.

Multi-Dwelling Units A set of properties that provide separate housing areas for more than one family but only require a single mortgage.

Multiple Listing Service A service that lists real estate offered for sale by a particular real estate agent that can be shown or sold by other real estate agents within a certain area.

National Association of Real Estate Investment Trusts (NAREIT) The national, non-profit trade organization that represents the real estate investment trust industry.

National Council of Real Estate Investment Fiduciaries (NCREIF) A group of real estate professionals who serve on committees; sponsor research articles, seminars and symposiums; and produce the NCREIF Property Index.

NCREIF Property Index (NPI) A quarterly and yearly report presenting income and appreciation components.

Negative Amortization An event that occurs when the deferred interest on an ARM is added, and the balance increases instead of decreases.

Net Asset Value (NAV) The total value of an asset or property minus leveraging or joint venture interests.

Net Asset Value Per Share The total value of a REIT's current assets divided by outstanding shares.

Net Assets The total value of assets minus total liabilities based on market value.

Net Cash Flow The total income generated by an investment property after expenses have been subtracted.

Net Investment in Real Estate Gross investment in properties minus the outstanding balance of debt.

Net Investment Income The income or loss of a portfolio or business minus all expenses, including portfolio and asset management fees, but before gains and losses on investments are considered.

Net Operating Income (NOI)
The pre-tax figure of gross revenue minus operating expenses and an allowance for expected vacancy.

Net Present Value (NPV) The sum of the total current value of incremental future cash flows plus the current value of estimated sales proceeds.

Net Purchase Price The gross purchase price minus any associated financed debt.

Net Real Estate Investment Value
The total market value of all real estate minus property-level debt.

Net Returns The returns paid to investors minus fees to advisers or managers.

Net Sales Proceeds The income from the sale of an asset, or part of an asset, minus brokerage commissions, closing costs, and market expenses.

Net Square Footage The total space required for a task or staff position.

Net Worth The worth of an individual or company figured on the basis of a difference between all assets and liabilities.

No-Cash-Out Refinance

Sometimes referred to as a Rate and Term Refinance. A refinancing transaction that is intended only to cover the balance due on the current loan and any costs associated with obtaining the new mortgage.

No-Cost Loan A loan for which there are no costs associated with the loan that are charged by the lender, but with a slightly higher interest rate.

No-Documentation Loan A type of loan application that requires no income or asset verification, usually granted based on strong credit with a large down payment.

Nominal Yield The yield investors receive before it is adjusted for fees, inflation, or risk.

Non-Assumption Clause A provision in a loan agreement that prohibits transferring a mortgage to another borrower without approval from the lender.

Non-Compete Clause A provision in a lease agreement that specifies that the tenant's business is the only one that may operate in the property in question, thereby preventing a competitor moving in next door.

Non-Conforming Loan Any

loan that is too large or does not meet certain qualifications to be purchased by Fannie Mae or Freddie Mac.

Non-Investment-Grade CMBS Also referred to as High-Yield CMBS. Commercial mortgage-backed securities that have ratings of BB or B.

Non-Performing Loan A loan agreement that cannot meet its contractual principal and interest payments.

Non-Recourse Debt A loan that limits the lender's options to collect on the value of the real estate in the event of a default by the borrower.

Nonrecurring Closing Costs Fees that are only paid one time in a given transaction.

Note A legal document requiring a borrower to repay a mortgage at a specified interest rate over a certain period of time.

Note Rate The interest rate that is defined in a mortgage note.

Notice of Default A formal written notification a borrower receives once the borrower is in default stating that legal action may be taken.

Offer A term that describes a

specified price or spread to sell whole loans or securities.

One-Year Adjustable-Rate Mortgage ARM for which the interest rate changes annually, generally based on movements of a published index and a specified margin.

Open Space A section of land or water that has been dedicated for public or private use or enjoyment.

Open-End Fund A type of commingled fund with an infinite life, always accepting new investor capital and making new investments in property.

Operating Expense The regular costs associated with operating and managing a property.

Option A condition in which the buyer pays for the right to purchase a property within a certain period of time without the obligation to buy.

Option ARM Loan A type of mortgage in which the borrower has a variety of payment options each month.

Original Principal Balance Total principal owed on a mortgage before a borrower has made a payment.

Origination Fee A fee that most lenders charge for the purpose of covering the costs associated with arranging the loan.

Originator A company that underwrites loans for commercial and/or multi-family properties.

Out-Parcel The individual retail sites located within a shopping center.

Overallotment A practice in which the underwriters offer and sell a higher number of shares than they had planned to purchase from the issuer.

Owner Financing A transaction in which the property seller agrees to finance all or part of the amount of the purchase.

Partial Payment An amount paid that is not large enough to cover the normal monthly payment on a mortgage loan.

Partial Sales The act of selling a real estate interest that is smaller than the whole property.

Partial Taking The appropriating of a portion of an owner's property under the laws of Eminent Domain.

Participating Debt Financing allowing the lender to have participatory rights to equity through increased income and/or residual value over the balance of

the loan or original value at the time the loan is funded.

Pass-Through Certificate A document that allows the holder to receive payments of principal and interest from the underlying pool of mortgages.

Payment Cap The maximum amount a monthly payment may increase on an ARM.

Payout Ratio Percentage of primary earnings per share, excluding unusual items, paid to common stockholders as cash dividends during the next 12 months.

Percentage Rent The amount of rent that is adjusted based on the percentage of gross sales or revenues the tenant receives.

Per-Diem Interest The interest that is charged or accrued daily.

Performance The changes each quarter in fund or account values that can be explained by investment income, realized or unrealized appreciation, and the total return to the investors before and after investment management fees.

Performance-Based Fees The fees that advisers or managers receive that are based on returns to investors.

271

Periodic Payment Cap The highest amount that payments can increase or decrease during a given adjustment period on an ARM.

Periodic Rate Cap The maximum amount that the interest rate can increase or decrease during a given adjustment period on an ARM.

Permanent Loan A long-term property mortgage.

PITI Principal, Interest, Taxes, Insurance. The items that are included in the monthly payment to the lender for an impounded loan, as well as mortgage insurance.

PITI Reserves The amount in cash that a borrower must readily have after the down payment and all closing costs are paid when purchasing a home.

Planned Unit Development (PUD) A type of ownership where individuals actually own the building or unit they live in, but common areas are owned jointly with the other members of the development or association. Contrast with condominium, where an individual actually owns the airspace of his unit, but the buildings and common areas are owned jointly with the others in the development or association.

Plat A chart or map of a certain area showing the boundaries of individual lots, streets, and easements.

Pledged Account Mortgage (PAM) A loan tied to a pledged savings account for which the fund and earned interest are used to gradually reduce mortgage payments.

Point Also referred to as a Discount Point. A fee a lender charges to provide a lower interest rate, equal to 1 percent of the amount of the loan.

Portfolio Management A process that involves formulating, modifying, and implementing a real estate investment strategy according to an investor's investment objectives.

Portfolio Turnover The amount of time averaged from the time an investment is funded until it is repaid or sold.

Power of Attorney A legal document that gives someone the authority to act on behalf of another party.

Power of Sale The clause included in a mortgage or deed of trust that provides the mortgagee (or trustee) with the right and power to advertise and sell the property at public auction if the borrower is in default.

Pre-Approval Complete analysis a lender makes regarding a potential borrower's ability to pay for a home as well as a confirmation of the proposed amount to be borrowed.

Pre-Approval Letter The letter a lender presents that states the amount of money they are willing to lend a potential buyer.

Pre-Leased A certain amount of space in a proposed building that must be leased before construction may begin or a certificate of occupancy may be issued.

Prepaid Expenses The amount of money that is paid before it is due, including taxes, insurance, and/or assessments.

Prepaid Fees The charges that a borrower must pay in advance regarding certain recurring items, such as interest, property taxes, hazard insurance, and PMI, if applicable.

Prepaid Interest The amount of interest that is paid before its due date.

Prepayment The money that is paid to reduce the principal balance of a loan before the date it is due.

Prepayment Penalty A penalty that may be charged to the borrower when he pays off a loan before the planned maturity date.

Prepayment Rights The right a borrower is given to pay the total principal balance before the maturity date free of penalty.

Prequalification Initial assessment by a lender of a potential borrower's ability to pay for a home as well as an estimate of how much the lender is willing to supply to the buyer.

Price-to-Earnings Ratio The comparison that is derived by dividing the current share price by the sum of the primary earnings per share from continuing operations over the past year.

Prime Rate The best interest rate reserved for a bank's preferred customers.

Prime Tenant The largest or highest-earning tenant in a building or shopping center.

Principal The amount of money originally borrowed in a mortgage, before interest is included and with any payments subtracted.

Principal Balance The total current balance of mortgage principal not including interest.

Principal Paid over Life of Loan The final total of scheduled payments to the principal that the lender calculates to equal the face amount of the loan.

Principal Payments The lender's return of invested capital.

Principle of Conformity The concept that a property will probably increase in value if its size, age, condition, and style are similar to other properties in the immediate area.

Private Equity A real estate investment that has been acquired by a noncommercial entity.

Private Mortgage Insurance (PMI) A type of policy that a lender requires when the borrower's down payment or home equity percentage is under 20 percent of the value of the property.

Private REIT Real estate investment company that is structured as a real estate investment trust that places and holds shares privately rather than publicly.

Pro Rata Proportionate amount of expenses per tenant for the property's maintenance and operation.

Processing Fee A fee some lenders charge for gathering the information necessary to process the loan.

Production Acres The portion of land that can be used directly in agriculture or timber activities to generate income, but not areas used for such things as machinery storage or support.

Prohibited Transaction Certain transactions that may not be performed between a pension plan and a party in interest, such as the following: the sale, exchange or lease of any property; a loan or other grant of credit; and furnishing goods or services.

Promissory Note Written agreement to repay a specific amount over a certain period of time.

Property Tax The tax that must be paid on private property.

Public Auction Announced public meeting held at a specified location for the purpose of selling property to repay a mortgage in default.

Public Debt Mortgages or other liabilities for which a commercial entity is responsible.

Public Equity A real estate investment that has been acquired by REITs and other publicly traded real estate operating companies.

Purchase Agreement Written contract buyer and seller both sign defining the terms and conditions under which a property is sold.

Purchase Money Transaction A transaction in which property is acquired through the exchange of money or something of equivalent value.

Purchase-Money Mortgage (PMM) A mortgage obtained by a borrower that serves as partial payment for a property.

Qualified Plan Any employee benefit plan that the IRS has approved as a tax-exempt plan.

Qualifying Ratio The measurement a lender uses to determine how much they are willing to lend to a potential buyer.

Quitclaim Deed A written document that releases a party from any interest they may have in a property.

Rate Cap The highest interest rate allowed on a monthly payment during an adjustment period of an ARM.

Rate Lock The commitment of a lender to a borrower that guarantees a certain interest rate for a specific amount of time.

Rate-Improvement Mortgage A loan that includes a clause that entitles a borrower to a one-time-only cut in the interest rate without having to refinance.

Rating Agencies Independent firms that are engaged to rate securities' creditworthiness on behalf of investors.

Rating A figure that represents the credit quality or creditworthiness of securities.

Raw Land A piece of property that has not been developed and remains in its natural state.

Raw Space Shell space in a building that has not yet been developed.

Real Estate Agent An individual who is licensed to negotiate and transact the real estate sales.

Real Estate Settlement Procedures Act (RESPA) A legislation for consumer protection that requires lenders to notify borrowers regarding closing costs in advance.

Real Property Land and anything else of a permanent nature that is affixed to the land.

Real Rate of Return The yield given to investors minus an inflationary factor.

Recorder A public official who records transactions that affect real estate in the area.

Recording The documentation that the registrar's office keeps of the details of properly executed legal documents.

Recording Fee A fee real estate agents charge for moving the sale of a piece of property into the public record.

Recourse Option a lender has for recovering losses against the personal assets of a secondary party who is also liable for a debt in default.

Refinance Transaction Act of paying off an existing loan using funding gained from a new loan that uses the same property as security.

Regional Diversification Boundaries that are defined based on geography or economic lines.

Registration Statement The set of forms that are filed with the SEC (or the appropriate state agency) regarding a proposed offering of new securities or the listing of outstanding securities on a national exchange.

Regulation Z A federal legislation under the Truth in Lending Act that requires lenders to advise the borrower in writing of all costs that are associated with the credit portion of a financial transaction.

Rehab Short for Rehabilitation. Refers to an extensive renovation intended to extend the life of a building or project.

Rehabilitation Mortgage A loan meant to fund the repairing and improving of a resale home or building.

Real Estate Investment Trust (REIT) A trust corporation that combines the capital of several investors for the purpose of acquiring or providing funding for real estate.

Remaining Balance The amount of the principal on a home loan that has not yet been paid.

Remaining Term The original term of the loan after the number of payments made has been subtracted.

Real Estate Mortgage Investment Conduit (REMIC) An investment vehicle that is designed to hold a pool of mortgages solely to issue multiple classes of mortgage-backed securities in a way that avoids doubled corporate tax.

Renewal Option A clause in a lease agreement that allows a tenant to extend the term of a lease.

Renewal Probability The average percentage of a building's tenants who are expected to renew terms at market rental rates upon the lease expiration.

Rent Loss Insurance A policy that covers loss of rent or rental value for a landlord due to any condition that renders the leased premises inhabitable, thereby excusing the tenant from paying rent.

Rent The fee paid for the occupancy and/or use of any rental property or equipment.

Rentable/Usable Ratio A total rentable area in a building divided by the area available for use.

Rental Growth Rate The projected trend of market rental rates over a particular period of analysis.

Rent-Up Period The period of time following completion of a new building when tenants are actively being sought and the project is stabilizing.

Real Estate Owned (REO) The real estate that a savings institution owns as a result of foreclosure on borrowers in default.

Repayment Plan An agreement made to repay late installments or advances.

Replacement Cost Projected cost by current standards of constructing a building that is equivalent to the building being appraised.

Replacement Reserve Fund Money that is set aside for replacing of common property in a condominium, PUD, or cooperative project.

Request for Proposal (RFP) A formal request that invites investment managers to submit information regarding investment strategies, historical investment performance, current investment opportunities, investment management fees, and other pension fund client relationships used by their firm.

Rescission The legal withdrawing of a contract or consent from the parties involved.

Reserve Account An account that must be funded by the borrower to protect the lender.

Retail Investor An investor who sells interests directly to consumers.

Retention Rate The percentage of trailing year's earnings that have been dispersed into the company again. It is calculated as 100 minus the trailing 12-month payout ratio.

Return on Assets The measurement of the ability to produce net profits efficiently by making use of assets.

Return on Equity Measurement of the return on the investment in a business or property.

Return on Investments The percentage of money that has been gained as a result of certain investments.

Reverse Mortgage See: Home Equity Conversion Mortgage.

Reversion Capitalization Rate The capitalization rate that is used to derive reversion value.

Reversion Value A benefit that an investor expects to receive as a lump sum at the end of an investment.

Revolving Debt A credit arrangement that enables a customer to borrow against a predetermined line of credit when purchasing goods and services.

Right of Ingress or Egress The option to enter or to leave the premises in question.

Right to Rescission A legal provision that enables borrowers to cancel certain loan types within three days after they sign.

Risk Management A logical approach to analyzing and defining insurable and non-insurable risks while evaluating the availability and costs of purchasing third-party insurance.

Risk-Adjusted Rate of Return A percentage that is used to identify investment options that are expected to deliver a positive premium despite their volatility.

Roll-Over Risk Possibility that tenants will not renew their lease.

Sale-Leaseback An arrangement in which a seller deeds a property, or part of it, to a buyer in exchange for money or the equivalent, then leases the property from the new owner.

Sales Comparison Value A value that is calculated by comparing the appraised property to similar properties in the area that have been recently sold.

Sales Contract Agreement both the buyer and seller sign defining the terms of a property sale.

Second Mortgage A secondary loan obtained on a piece of property.

Secondary Market A market in which existing mortgages are bought and sold as part of a mortgages pool.

Second-Generation or Secondary Space Space that has been occupied before and becomes available for lease again, either by the landlord or as a sublease.

Secured Loan A loan that is secured by some sort of collateral.

Security Property or other asset that will serve as a loan's collateral.

Security Deposit An amount of money a tenant gives to a landlord to secure the performance of terms in a lease agreement.

Seisen (Seizen) The ownership of real property under a claim of freehold estate.

Self-Administered REIT A REIT in which the management are employees of the REIT or similar entity.

Seller Carry-Back An arrangement in which the seller provides the financing to purchase a home.

Seller Financing A type of funding in which the borrower may use part of the equity in the property to finance the purchase.

Separate Account A relationship in which a single pension plan sponsor is used to retain an investment manager or adviser under a stated investment policy exclusively for that sponsor.

Servicer An organization that collects principal and interest payments from borrowers and manages borrowers' escrow accounts on behalf of a trustee.

Servicing The process of collecting mortgage payments from borrowers as well as related responsibilities.

Setback The distance required from a given reference point before a structure can be built.

Settlement or Closing Fees The fees that the escrow agent receives for carrying out the written instructions in the agreement between borrower and lender and/ or buyer and seller.

Shared-Appreciation Mortgage A loan that enables a lender or other party to share in the profits of the borrower when the borrower sells the home.

Shared-Equity Transaction A transaction in which two people purchase a property, one as a residence and the other as an investment.

Site Analysis A determination of how suitable a specific parcel of land is for a particular use.

Site Development Implementation of all improvements needed for a site before construction may begin.

Site Plan A detailed description and map of the location of improvements to a parcel.

Slab Flat, exposed surface laid over the structural support beams to form the building's floor(s).

Soft Cost Part of an equity investment, aside from the literal cost of the improvements, that could be tax-deductible in the first year.

Special Assessment Certain charges that are levied against real estates for public improvements to benefit the property in question.

Special Servicer A company that is hired to collect on mortgages that are either delinquent or in default.

Specified Investing A strategy of investment in individually specified properties, portfolios, or commingled funds are fully or partially detailed prior to the commitment of investor capital.

Stabilized Net Operating Income Expected income minus expenses that reflect relatively stable operations.

Stabilized Occupancy The best projected range of long-term occupancy that a piece of rental property will achieve after existing in the open market for a reasonable period of time with terms and conditions that are comparable to similar offerings.

Step-Rate Mortgage A loan that allows for a gradual interest rate increase during the first few years of the loan.

Step-Up Lease (Graded Lease) A lease agreement that specifies certain increases in rent at certain intervals during the complete term of the lease.

Straight Lease (Flat Lease) Lease agreement that specifies an amount of rent that should be paid regularly during the complete term of the lease.

Subcontractor A contractor who has been hired by the general contractor, often specializing in a certain required task for the construction project.

Subdivision Most common type of housing development created by dividing a larger tract of land into individual lots for sale or lease.

Sublessee A person or business that holds the rights of use and occupancy under a lease contract with the original lessee, who still retains primary responsibility for the lease obligations.

Subordinate Financing Any loan with a priority lower than loans that were obtained beforehand.

Subordinate Loan A second or third mortgage obtained with the same property being used as collateral.

Subordinated Classes Classes that have the lowest priority of receiving payments from underlying mortgage loans.

Subordination The act of sharing credit loss risk at varying rates among two or more classes of securities.

Subsequent Rate Adjustments Interest rate for ARMs that adjusts at regular intervals, sometimes differing from the duration period of the initial interest rate.

Subsequent Rate Cap Maximum amount the interest rate may increase at each regularly scheduled interest rate adjustment date on an ARM.

Survey A document or analysis containing the precise measurements of a piece of property as performed by a licensed surveyor.

Sweat Equity The non-cash improvements in value that an owner adds to a piece of property.

Synthetic Lease A transaction that is considered to be a lease by accounting standards but a loan by tax standards.

Taking Similar to condemning, or any other interference with rights to private property, but a physical seizure or appropriation is not required.

Tax Base The determined value of all property that lies within the jurisdiction of the taxing authority.

Tax Lien A type of lien placed against a property if the owner has not paid property or personal taxes.

Tax Roll Record that contains the descriptions of all land parcels and their owners that is located within the county.

Tax Service Fee A fee that is charged for the purpose of setting up monitoring of the borrower's property tax payments by a third party.

Teaser Rate A small, short-term interest rate offered on a mortgage in order to convince the potential borrower to apply.

Tenancy by the Entirety A form of   281

ownership held by spouses in which they both hold title to the entire property with right of survivorship.

Tenancy in Common A type of ownership held by two or more owners in an undivided interest in the property with no right of survivorship.

Tenant (Lessee) A party who rents a piece of real estate from another by way of a lease agreement.

Tenant at Will A person who possesses a piece of real estate with the owner's permission.

Tenant Improvement (TI) Allowance The specified amount of money that the landlord contributes toward tenant improvements.

Tenant Improvement (TI) The upgrades or repairs that are made to the leased premises by or for a tenant.

Tenant Mix The quality of the income stream for a property.

Term Length that a loan lasts or is expected to last before it is repaid.

Third-Party Origination Process in which another party is used by the lender to originate, process, underwrite, close, fund, or package the mortgages it expects to deliver to the secondary mortgage market.

Timeshare A form of ownership involving purchasing a specific period of time or percentage of interest in a vacation property.

Time-Weighted Average Annual Rate of Return The regular yearly return over several years that would have the same return value as combining the actual annual returns for each year in the series.

Title The legal written document that provides someone ownership in a piece of real estate.

Title Company A business that determines that a property title is clear and that provides title insurance.

Title Exam An analysis of the public records in order to confirm that the seller is the legal owner, and there are no encumbrances on the property.

Title Insurance Type of policy issued to both lenders and buyers to cover loss due to property ownership disputes that may arise at a later date.

Title Insurance Binder A written promise from the title insurance company to insure the title to the property, based on the conditions and exclusions shown in the binder.

Title Risk The potential

impediments in transferring a title from one party to another.

Title Search The process of analyzing all transactions existing in the public record in order to determine whether any title defects could interfere with the clear transfer of property ownership.

Total Acres The complete amount of land area that is contained within a real estate investment.

Total Assets The final amount of all gross investments, cash and equivalents, receivables, and other assets as they are presented on the balance sheet.

Total Commitment The complete funding amount that is promised once all specified conditions have been met.

Total Expense Ratio The comparison of monthly debt obligations to gross monthly income.

Total Inventory The total amount of square footage commanded by property within a geographical area.

Total Lender Fees Charges that the lender requires for obtaining the loan, aside from other fees associated with the transfer of a property.

Total Loan Amount The basic amount of the loan plus any additional financed closing costs.

Total Monthly Housing Costs The amount that must be paid each month to cover principal, interest, property taxes, PMI, and/or either hazard insurance or homeowners' association dues.

Total of All Payments The total cost of the loan after figuring the sum of all monthly interest payments.

Total Principal Balance The sum of all debt, including the original loan amount adjusted for subsequent payments and any unpaid items that may be included in the principal balance by the mortgage note or by law.

Total Retail Area Total floor area of a retail center that is currently leased or available for lease.

Total Return The final amount of income and appreciation returns per quarter.

Townhouse An attached home that is not considered to be a condominium.

Trade Fixtures Any personal property that is attached to a structure and used in the business but is removable once the lease is terminated.

Trading Down Act of purchasing a property that is less expensive than the one currently owned.

Trading Up The act of purchasing a property that is more expensive than the one currently owned.

TransUnion Corporation One of the primary credit-reporting bureaus.

Transfer of Ownership Any process in which a property changes hands from one owner to another.

Transfer Tax An amount specified by state or local authorities when ownership in a piece of property changes hands.

Triple Net Lease A lease that requires the tenant to pay all property expenses on top of the rental payments.

Trustee A fiduciary who oversees property or funds on behalf of another party.

Truth-in-Lending The federal legislation requiring lenders to fully disclose the terms and conditions of a mortgage in writing.

Two- to Four-Family Property A structure that provides living space for two to four families while ownership is held in a single deed.

Two-Step Mortgage An ARM with two different interest rates: one for the loan's first five or seven years and another for the remainder of the loan term.

Under Contract The period of time during which a buyer's offer to purchase a property has been accepted, and the buyer is able to finalize financing arrangements without the concern of the seller making a deal with another buyer.

Underwriter A company, usually an investment banking firm, that is involved in a guarantee that an entire issue of stocks or bonds will be purchased.

Underwriting The process during which lenders analyze the risks a particular borrower presents and set appropriate conditions for the loan.

Underwriting Fee A fee that mortgage lenders charge for verifying the information on the loan application and making a final decision on approving the loan.

Unencumbered A term that refers to property free of liens or other encumbrances.

Unimproved Land See: Raw Land.

Unrecorded Deed A deed that transfers right of ownership from one owner to another without being officially documented.

Umbrella Partnership Real Estate Investment Trust (UPREIT) An organizational structure in which a REIT's assets are owned by a holding company for tax reasons.

Usable Square Footage The total area that is included within the exterior walls of the tenant's space.

VA Loan A mortgage through the VA program in which a down payment is not necessarily required.

Vacancy Factor The percentage of gross revenue that pro-forma income statements expect to be lost due to vacancies.

Vacancy Rate The percentage of space that is available to rent.

Vacant Space Existing rental space that is presently being marketed for lease minus space that is available for sublease.

Value-Added A phrase advisers and managers generally use to describe investments in underperforming and/or under-managed assets.

Variable Rate Mortgage (VRM) A loan in which the interest rate changes according to fluctuations in particular indexes.

Variable Rate Also called adjustable rate. The interest rate on a loan that varies over the term of the loan according to a predetermined index.

Variance A permission that enables a property owner to work around a zoning ordinance's literal requirements which cause a unique hardship due to special circumstances.

Verification of Deposit (VOD) The confirmation statement a borrower's bank may be asked to sign in order to verify the borrower's account balances and history.

Verification of Employment (VOE) The confirmation statement a borrower's employer may be asked to sign in order to verify the borrower's position and salary.

Veterans Affairs (VA) A federal government agency that assists veterans in purchasing a home without a down payment.

Waiting Period The period of time between initially filing a registration statement and the date it becomes effective.

Warehouse Fee A closing cost

fee that represents the lender's expense of temporarily holding a borrower's loan before it is sold on the secondary mortgage market.

Weighted-Average Coupon The average, using the balance of each mortgage as the weighting factor, of the gross interest rates of the mortgages underlying a pool as of the date of issue.

Weighted-Average Equity The part of the equation that is used to calculate investment-level income, appreciation, and total returns on a quarter-by-quarter basis.

Weighted-Average Rental Rates The average ratio of unequal rental rates across two or more buildings in a market.

Working Drawings The detailed blueprints for a construction project that comprise the contractual documents which describe the exact manner in which a project is to be built.

Wraparound Mortgage A loan obtained by a buyer to use for the remaining balance on the seller's first mortgage, as well as an additional amount requested by the seller.

Write-Down A procedure used in accounting when an asset's book value is adjusted downward to reflect current market value more accurately.

Write-Off A procedure used in accounting when an asset is determined to be uncollectible and is therefore considered to be a loss.

Yield Maintenance Premium A penalty the borrower must pay in order to make investors whole in the event of early repayment of principal.

Yield Spread The difference in income derived from a commercial mortgage and from a benchmark value.

Yield The actual return on an investment, usually paid in dividends or interest.

Zoning Ordinance The regulations and laws that control the use or improvement of land in a particular area or zone.

Zoning The act of dividing a city or town into particular areas and applying laws and regulations regarding the architectural design, structure, and intended uses of buildings within those areas.

INDEX